It's Hard to be a Woman

ALPHA VILLANEA

This Book is a work of nonfiction.

Ordering Information:

Prime Seven Media
518 Landmann St.
Tomah City, WI 54660

Printed in the United States of America

Table of Contents

//

Chapter 1

(Philippines)

With confidence and poise, I presented my thesis to the panel, my nerves transformed into energized enthusiasm. Despite nervous energy I tried to keep my voice steady. I channelled my nerves into a powerful presentation. The panel's applause is music to my ears. Ms. Judy approached, with her radiant smile "your vision for a beach resort is truly inspiring" beaming with pride as she shook my hand. "Your professionalism shines through, and those shoes are the perfect finishing touch! With her winking eye. The panelist followed, offering warm congratulations and handshakes. One by one offering sincere words of praise, As I gazed at the impressive mark on my folder, a reflection of my hardwork and determination.

One cloudy Sunday morning, and it's a day of spiritual rejuvenation and cherished family moments! As I make my way downstairs, I'm met with the heart warming sight of my Dad. His humble attire, a plain polo shirt with a cigarette pocket and off white khaki pants paired with a customized leather sandals reflects his down-to-earth nature. With bright smiles I showered him with hugs and kisses on his cheek "good morning daddy, I love you" I exclaim.

As I sat before him, he asked "do you need something?" I reply "not at all, I just miss you; life has been a journey lately". We share a hearty laugh, basking in the warmth of the moment.

As I glance at the time, fifteen minutes have passed, and my older brother and younger sister are sitting alongside me. "I should go check on Rena", I say, rushing upstairs, where I can hear my son's gleeful giggles.

I open the door and I find Rena dressed up as my four-year-old daughter and my six year-old-son playing with baby powder covering his face with white mess. "Mommy, look, I'm a white monster, grrrrr!" he exclaims as I laugh and cuddle him up to my waist. I tap Rena shoulder "thank you i'll take it from here" before long, we're ready. With Alex securely in her carrier and Jacob eagerly running to grandpa, his tiny hands holding on to grandpa's "Lolo, we're ready". My Dad sweetly laughs "ok, let's go!". Off we go to our red jeep.

Mass leaves us feeling refreshed and ready to embrace the week filled with a sense of renewal and purpose. Our favorite part is our lunch together at our go-to restaurant, a time we make memories and our family tradition that uplifts us. Although my mom's move to New York six years ago was tough, her relocation gives us strength in our togetherness.

One week of classes remains before graduation day. As I enter the school gate, my friends are lined up on a bench. Louise exclaims "you're finally here!" and they sprint towards me, dragging me out. We head to picardals, naughtily laughing. I struggled to keep up with my heels and tight skirt. "Slow down you guys, I might wreck my skirt" giggling as they kept dragging me. Darlene teases, "who cares about our uniforms, we won't be wearing them again!" my jaw dropped, after hearing her statement "am I seriously hearing this from the daughter of the owner of the school?" We all hilariously laughed. We gathered at our usual table at a sari-sari store, enjoying our favorite snacks and Tanduay rum. Reminiscing about our four years together.

Darlene loves to do the 'tagay' delegating shot glasses, which she claims she's expert at, making sure everyone drinks every shot, no one shall pass. Donna came in the gate in her nursing uniform, took out a pack of Marlboro reds, placed it on the center table, lighting one stick for herself; and I lit one for me. Our large group as usual is the loudest among the crowd.

Time flies and it's already ten in the evening; the store is closing after a few drinks, but the party doesn't stop there. Darlene wants to keep drinking and play pool, so we head to hard nine, a pub where we can drink and smoke inside. The owner always accommodates us, even in uniform, since we're regular customers. We drink to our heart's content and head home at two in the morning.

It's past nine in the evening, with my children sleeping soundly, I seize the opportunity for a night out with the 'barkadas'. Our nanny Rena, is still wide awake, reading Tagalog pocketbooks by the make up dresser.

I whisper to her, I'm going out, please call me on my cell if something comes up; I'm wearing skinny faded jeans, a black lace halter top and classic strappy black wedges. I planted love and kisses to both my angels and I tiptoed out of our room gently closing the door behind me.

At the nightclub, my gay best friend greets me with a bottle of san miguel lights. I placed my purse in our group table. Sam passed me a tequila shot "shot! shot! para igat" giggling with her last two words then chug the shot glass "whooww! that burnsss! haha!". We dance the night away, letting loose like theres no tomorrow.

After the waiter cleared our table, I took my wedge off to climb up at the top table and gracefully dancing people started crowding the table and dancing along. One man I don't know climbed up the top table and pulled me closer to him. I swiftly swung around behind him whispering in his ears "sorry I like to dance alone, get off my table" gently pushing him out. He stood down in front of the table staring for a long time naughtily smiling.

———— ////////// ————

As sunlight streams through my bedroom window, warming my face, a loud clanging on the wall jolts me awake. Jacob, drop that! I shout, Jacob holding a broken sharp rattle; leaping out of bed and tossing the broken rattle to the floor. Jacob erupts into tears.

I scoop him up, cradling him on my hip and gently swaying to soothe him. A knock at the door interrupts us. "Come In!" I called out, wondering "is that you dad?" Grandma enters with a smile. "Good morning, everyone" Jacob spots her and rushes to the door, squealing "Grandma!".

Jacob twirled a blue straw in his sippy cup while mischievously munching his hotdog. Grandma was peeling a ripe mango, slicing it into thin strips and placing them on Alex's plate. Meanwhile, I sat close by sipping my tea. "Well, somebody is going to get spoiled today," I said, winking to grandma. "Why don't you go relax, I've got this" she gestured for me to leave, so I grabbed my tea and book and walked to the living room, slouching on the red velvet couch and opening my book to chapter six.

Three months into my role as a front desk clerk at the top hotel in our city, our manager's morning greeting became familiar: "beautiful morning to all, have a wonderful day and keep smiling, even on the craziest days- we can do this!" Then we cheer each other on and head to our assigned departments.

Today's a busy day, and I'm racing to finish urgent reports. Non-stop check ins and check outs have filled my schedule, and it's after two in the afternoon I still haven't taken a lunch break and my stomach is protesting.

Ben, one of the waiters, approached the front desk, saying "hey Alpha, I'll watch the desk; go take your lunch" smiling brightly, I immediately grabbed my purse. "Thank you Ben, you're a lifesaver," I said, heading out the door wearing black heeled shoes that showed off my sexy legs, a silky blouse, and my long wavy black hair flowing behind me. Feeling glamorous with my cat-eye metal trim sunglasses, walking down the street toward my favorite Chowking restaurant.

As I entered the restaurant, I was greeted immediately by a friendly server whom I see all the time whenever I eat here. "Hello miss Alpha" she said warmly smiling as she took the food tray from the counter "having your usual?" cheerfully asking; I smiled replying "yes, my usual please" after taking my order and payment, I praised her saying "wow, you never cease to amaze me, working hard student, she nodded saying "well, somebody got to" then she let's me know "you're order will be ready in fifteen minutes. I gave her a thumbs up and sat at my favorite corner spot.

Sitting in a cold air-conditioned restaurant, I can feel the outside heat as I observe the bustling street. Jeepneys zip by, packed with passengers. Across the street, small stalls offer assorted goods. A fabric stall is crowded, while a beauty products stall beside it attracts women of all ages with bags full of makeup coming out the store. By the corner, a small repair shop has a steady stream of clients bringing items like bags, shoes, watches, picture frames, bread toasters, TVs, and microwaves to be fixed by an elderly hunchbacked man. It's fascinating to watch people go about their day.

"Lunch served to a lovely woman, who always sits by this corner window" my nose took a whiff of the delicious chao fan rice, pork roll, and steamed kang kong with shrimp paste topping. We exchange warm smiles and laughter with a "thank you". Place the cold ice tea "bon appetit".

As I enjoyed my meal, I noticed a pair of eyes on me. Looking over my shoulder, I saw a stranger in a gray suit sipping coffee. His eyes gleamed as they locked onto mine; he smiled and tossed his mug, saying "cheers". I ignored him, finished my meal, grabbed my ice-cold tea, and left for the hotel.

Ben approached me hastily at the entrance door and handed me a clipboard. "The boss wants you to know that a VIP guest is arriving today;please double check our premium room" After taking the clipboard, I put on my blazer, smoothed my hair, and tied it into a ponytail before rushing to the elevator and heading to the twelfth floor, where I paused to collect myself.

An hour and a half remains before clocking. The VIP room is spotless and clean. The large conference group of electrical engineers has finished for the day, attracting over two hundred participants from different provinces. The night shift waiters are now preparing dinner. After completing the VIP paper work, I went to the kitchen to lend a hand. Four waiters, carrying large chafing dishes, entered the restaurant, accompanied by five trainee students carrying dinner plates, cutlery, and dessert plates.

Wearing the black apron, I swiftly grabbed a full tray of sodas and went inside the conference room, placing coke bottles on every large group of tables. The tunes playing made the whole crew grooving along while working hard, bringing smiles to our guest's despite the crazy busy moment. After everyone was served and sitting in their places, enjoying every bite, the security waving from the glass window signaled to me that a guest was approaching.

After smoothing my hair and adjusting my uniform, I walked behind the desk and smiled warmly. I froze for a second, gazing fixed on the VIP guest before me. To my surprise! It was the same man from the restaurant earlier, who smiled charmingly and said "hello we meet again" winking at me who was accompanied by two armed men.

"Hello and welcome to Eve hotel, have a wonderful stay with us". She handed him two room keys. "Should you need anything else, please notify the front desk". Once the three gentlemen entered the elevator, I exhaled heavily. "Now I can finally go home to my children".

I arrived home after seven in the evening. Upon entering the gate, I heard the lively commotion from the living room- Jacob's mischievous laughter and Alex playfully banging her rattle and yelling at her brother. As I opened the front door, carrying groceries, I greeted my family. "Hello, my angels!" Jacob rushed over, "Mommy! mommy! you're home!" tightly hugging into my legs. He is always excited to help in taking off my shoes and putting on slippers, I cuddled Alex, who showered me with kisses drooling over my face. The scent of fresh milk was lovely. Meanwhile, Grandma sat comfortably on the couch, flipping through her fan. I gently hold up her right hand, bowing and touching my forehead to the back of her right hand. "Thank you Lola" she brightly smiled "bless you my apo".

Every Sunday, Jack collects Jacob and Alex. He usually waits by the lawn. They attend church and spend time with their grandparents and whole family on their father's side. Despite what happened between us I want my children to grow knowing who their father is.

It pains me greatly whenever Jack brings Alex back and Jacob goes with them. The separation of my two children causes me immense pain, a lifelong agony. I pray and trust God that one day they will reunite and no longer grow apart from each other. After dropping Alex off, Jack is always in a hurry to return home to their province. My bonding time with my son is always short leaving us with insufficient time to bond with him.

My dad love's coffee, I often find him sipping at the dining table. He affectionately calls my daughter Alex, who loves giving him sloppy kisses on the cheek. He always comments, " we can never spend a long time with Jacob". It's a painful statement I don't know how to respond to; "I know Dad, it's ok I will get to see him again next weekend.

Two months have passed since Rena went back to school, and we've had no nanny. I am juggling caring for my mentally handicapped daughter, cooking, cleaning, laundry and work demands feels never-ending. Im grateful to have a supportive dad and a grandma who helps look after Alex occasionally, even if she's busy caring for her newborn apo; my mom's sister, who lives with us, just had a baby two weeks ago, but Lola still manages to lend a bit of help when I need it.

Mondays are the day Alex visits her psychiatrist for a two-hour session doing motional therapy and behavioural therapy. A very expensive service Alex must do. Thankfully I am blessed with my mother's financial support. I am able to afford to bring my daughter every session since I don't get any financial help from her father.

One week off from work flew by quickly. The first day back felt too long. Ben smiling widely as I step inside the desk "what's up Ben? what's with this look?" teasing smile "someone here has been so eager to see you again" giving him rolling eyes "I know must be sir Ernie wants to give me more tasks to do" laughing at my own statement "ahh! Ah! No no" making his funny gay gesture finger, I'm raising my eyebrow with curiosity "who is it?" raising his left shoulder and turning away "you'll see I'm going back to work now byeee" giving me his teasing smile again.

Too focused on looking at the logbook checking every reservation and booking events coming up then I noticed a man's shadow on my desk. I look up and see our VIP guest. "ohh hello good morning sir, are you ready to check out?" clears his throat "no, I'm extending my stay for another week" "of course here let me update your room keys, glad you had a great stay with us" here you go, handing the updated room keys and he slips a piece of blank paper on top of my desk "if it's ok can I please have your number" the unexpected request got me loss for a moment "ohh yeah" writing down our landline number.

His charming smile showed off as he slid the paper in his pocket "thank you, I'll see you soon Ms. Alpha Villanea, right?" confirming my full name "yes Mr. Jake Fernandez?" stammering in response "have a wonderful day sir".

All room attendants are busy, two people called and sick short staff like today gets me going. Few rooms calling for amenities, no one is available to do the task. I'm running up and down the elevator delivering every room. Phone ringing from the banquet

"Alpha, we need help I'm down with one server" "ok ill be right up" I left the desk for the security guard to watch and to call me when I'm needed.

I sat for a second massaging my foot. I have been running around all day. I glanced at my watch for half an hour and I'll call it a day. I shoot a text to my best friend Cassey *"I totally need a drink after a long day like this you down tonight? Nine bars?"* gracefully walking back to my desk. The phone vibrated with Cassey's response *"yes! See you there at nine".*

After bathe I put Alex to bed turning the lullaby music she loves. Thankfully grandma sleeping over tonight is perfect timing for my evening plan. Dried my hair letting my curls go put a faded skinny jeans, black halter top cover up with a black leather jacket pairing a platform floral wedge.

Dad is sitting by his window, enjoying a movie, when I stop by to bid him farewell. "Hi Dad, sorry to interrupt, I'm leaving now- Louise is here". He swiftly rises and walks me out, embodying his steadfast parental care. My father's insistence on meeting my companions stems from his profound love and desire to protect me. I may perceive it as overprotectiveness, his flexibility in letting me go out with trusted individuals showcases his trust. A memorable experience was when I attended a beach party without informing him of my overnight stay; the lack of phone signal led to worry, almost prompting him to search for me. This moment underscores his unwavering commitment to my safety and well-being.

Upon entering the lively bar, I'm greeted by Casseys radiant smile and contagious laughter, her red horse beer raised high as she dances to the beat. We secure a cozy corner table, where friends are having fun engaged in a game of billiards. Louise kindly offers me a rum mix with coke. Embracing the moment, I attempt to play billiards, despite my inexperience. After four glasses of rum, my focus blurs, but my enthusiasm remains. "Hey Cassey, how many balls remain on the table?" The gang burst into laughter at my question "Don't rely on me; my counting skills are compromised after several beers!" We all erupt in joyful laughter.

After two at dawn, we stroll across the street to a twenty-four-hour haven, sipping coffee before heading home. Gazing out the window, watching the bustling nightlife, I'm reminded of life's beauty. A familiar figure sits beside me "we meet again, Alpha" a voice says. Turning, I see him sitting comfortably, his peaceful nature is infectious, inviting reflection.

"I have been watching you and your friends having a great time at the bar" flipping my hair backwards facing him "what a businessman like you doing in a bar at this late of time?" sarcastically smiled "what about you? A beautiful woman who is going to work in six hours from now doing out late?".

Louise and Cassey came at once and overheard what Jake said "ohhh hello my name is Louise and this is Cassey and we are the bff of this lovely lady and you are?" extending his hand "Jake Fernandez, pleasure to meet you both" earnestly handshaking.

After an hour of chatting Jake nicely offered "may I offer to drive you all home?" Louise pinch my leg "hey, aww" with his drunken smile "you know Cassey and I are good will grab a taxi why don't you bring our lovely friend here home safe and sound, just a warning of her dad" Louise swiftly smacking on my check and Cassey throwing me a hug "bye! have wonderful time" marching out the door before I spit a out a word. "Seriously you guys" "well guess your friends trust me enough to bring you home, shall we". Walking out the door and leading me towards his BMW.

The twenty-minute drive home went by quickly. Unlocking the seat belt "thank you, I guess ill see you at work in few hours?" he sweetly smiled and said "yes! looking forward to see you in a few". Hi eyes glistening as I step out the car.

My head was spinning while preparing breakfast for Alex, with her special diet that I personally wanted to make as her psychiatrist suggested. Time is getting too tight for me to get ready for work, constantly glancing at the wall clock. I stepped into the frontdesk office at seven forty-five with a heavy headache. "Good morning Alpha" I snapped out of my dizziness, my nose catching a whiff of brewed coffee. There he was, standing in front of me, looking ravishing in his faded jeans and plain white shirt, handing me a coffee cup. "Thought this may help start your day" he said. Lost for words with my frozen brain, I stammered, "thank you". I'm free today and I would like to invite you for dinner later, hoping you can show me around the city too?" With alcohol still running through my nerves, I politely accepted his invitation: "yes, it'll be my pleasure, sir Jack". "Perfect! It's a date. I'll pick you up at six tonight".

We dine at one of my favorite restaurants in town, nothing fancy. The place is simple, but the ambience always feels cozy, and it's my family's go-to spot for special occasions. We sat in silence while deciding what's on the menu.

"What is your favorite here?" he asked sweetly. "I love the *sotanghon guisado;* it has a unique taste you should try". he laid the menu on the table. "Tell you what, let's order your favorites". I stared at him for a second. "You might not like what I like". I noticed his dimples as he smiled. "You will find out later; I'm really trying hard to impress this lovely woman,"he said, turning his head towards the server. I smirked at his statement. "Right, if such a compliment is true, the father of my children wouldn't be out there hunting other lovely women in town". "Well, I'd say it's his loss, and let's not ruin this beautiful evening by mentioning him". I felt his genuine statement, and just like that, one wonderful evening went by perfectly fast.

Two years later, Jack became a part of the family, although he kept travelling for business trips; our communication remained constant. It took a long time for me to introduce him formally to my children and family, but he was very patient and waited for my decision.

It's always a transformative experience whenever I travel to Manila. I'm empowered by the resilience of its people amidst bumper-to-bumper traffic. I always stay at my aunt's, but Jack's driver picks me up from the airport and drives me to certain places I need to go. I decided to pursue my passion and put up a restaurant in our town. I wanted to learn the business, so I signed up for a business symposium conducted in Manila for five days; after each session I get to spend time with Jack.

Before my flight back to Iligan, we decided to spend my last two days in one of the breathtaking beach resorts in Batangas, creating unforgettable memories. Although over the last two years has been more of a long distance relationship, our constant communication has been the foundation of our bond, and we seize every opportunity to travel and meet each other, cherishing every precious moment together.

A serene haven to rejuvenate and break free from the chaos of daily life and work. With a flowing pool waters blend seamlessly into the vibrant blue waters of the seas and clear blue skies converge with the seas. A paradise that leaves incredible memories during your stay.

We booked a modern luxurious king bedroom with the pool and garden views, a marble bathroom, premium toiletries fifty-inch smart tv wireless internet. Opening the wide curtain glass window embracing the sun kissing my face. I inhaled deeply and let out a big exhale. "wooww this is heaven" Jack standing behind me wrapping his arm around my waist pressing his cheek to mine both of us fascinated by this paradise.

While night is young sipping our cocktails at the bar located in the center of the pool while enjoying the exquisite view of the beach. Night is crawling in and we have the delightful experience in the most sumptuous cuisines from a delicious local taste to a perfect international feast is a must to try.

As we returned to our room, locking the door behind us, Jack enveloped me in a tender embrace holding me close to his heart; he whispered in my ear; "I cherish you so deeply, hon, it's filling me with joy". "I cherish you too". Our lips met in a loving kiss and our spirits soared; his hand gently explored the depths inside of my bikini to the connection between us running wild. He lifted me in his arms, laying me on the bed with care. I felt his hardness in between my legs, my body screaming for more of him, my tongue explored the vastness of his manhood. My brain went wilder; pushing him down climbing on top of him intensely swaying my whole being, I am running out of breath as my womanhood sucking up the hardness out of him. His strong right arm lifted me up, flipping me on my back; grabbing my hair as he strongly entered behind me; screaming in pleasure as he intensely thrusting deeper inside my wonders; "aaahhhh!! more!more honnn!!! deeper!" shouting and begging until we both scream in delight as we reach our satisfaction. Our enchanting night left us both serene; and drifted off to sleep, wrapped in each other's loving arms.

Whenever I get the chance to travel, one place I look forward to visiting is a church. I went to one popular church, known as Quiapo church, or the minor basilica church of the black Nazarene. I couldn't help but admire its unique architectural design. An old lady was kneeling in the very front altar with a white knitted cloth on her head. A group of students in their school uniforms were busy chatting in hushed tones. I sat in an empty pose kneeled and solemnly prayed.

One hour and a half travel from the airport killed my back. Dad is standing in front of our white gate holding to the railings assuming he's waiting for me. I paid the taxi to grab my luggage and my father opened the gate for me. "Welcome home thank God for your safe travel" blessing his hand "thanks Dad, miss you all" glad to see Jacob home playing with Alex "miss you mommy!" endless embrace to both my angels. "Alpha once you settle in come see me in my room" glance around to face dad he sounds serious "ok dad see you in bit".

Basketball game is playing on TV, standing by the door and Dad is sitting in his favorite chair watching his favorite game show "hi dad you want me to come back later? I know how much you don't want to miss this game?" He took the remote and turned the television off. "it's ok I can watch the reply later, sit down" I felt I have done something wrong with his acting. Opened his drawer and took a white envelope. "Remember what I keep telling you be careful what you pray for because you might get it, and if God grants it don't complain" arousing curiosity "what is it dad?"

Handed me the letter "read it, and congratulations" without hesitation I immediately read it; it's from the agency I applied to work in Canada from two years ago. "What? I have forgotten about this it's been so long" "it's a great opportunity for you and the children, think of your children's future" "it says here Dad that I have to leave in a month too short notice" "you prayed for it now you have it, don't complain remember to thank God for it" mix emotions run over me happy, sad, worried and excited "thank you, love you daddy".

Sat by the window, the moon shining brightly, stars sparkling in the night sky. Sipping a second bottle of San Miguel lights staring at my two children sleeping soundly glancing at the letter by the edge of the bed. My mind is blowing with the choice I need to make.

In teary eyes Ernie holding the resignation letter "I'm sorry for the short notice, I have only given a month to prepare before leaving Philippines" endless hand shaking "you will be missed and congratulations" "thank you sir I learned so much in my years working here this is like my second home and family here". Heavy legs walking out the hotel after saying goodbyes to everyone.

Dad laid in the sand, my sister holding a hand scooper shoveling sand along with Jacob and Alex scooping wet sand covering dad's whole body except the head. The sound of the beach waves brings soothing peaceful feelings within. Jack brings in the mixed seafood BBQs, him and my brother cook. A perfect sunny Saturday by the sea with family one more week and off I fly to a new country starting a life of unknown.

An old man about in his sixties came by our open cottage with a bucket full of *chocolate moron* "ma'am you want to buy for the kids" smiling joyfully "Lo, i'll buy it for me! how much is all that?" flinging hands in happiness, I step closer and hug this poor old man working hard at his age "Lo, you should call it a day we will enjoy this suman" "ma'am thank you" holding to my palms tightly "Lo, just call me Alpha come joins us for lunch there's plenty for everyone what's your name Lo?" "Cannor ma'am" laugh at his response "Lo, I said just Alpha, no ma'am" Jack handed him a plate kissing me on the forehead peeling a chocolate moron lovingly sticking it to my mouth "I know it's your favorite hon, your big heart never fails to make me love you more" wobbling the sweet, delicious moron "there's no one like me so don't even think of doing stupid things when were already worlds apart". Everybody burst into laughter.

We are all gathered in the living room with two large luggage by the front door. Embracing Jacob and Alex tightly "mommy come back soon ok" a request from my innocent eight-year-old son "I love you both so much, I will miss you every second's pass". Squeezing cuddling dad dearly "I love you dad I will call everyday promise". "No goodbyes, till I see you all again soon". Rolling out the door, pressing palms firmly to my luggage, weak knees stepping out the gate.

With my big brother and first cousin Han and my amazing aunt Lilet came with me to Manila International Airport "here's a gift for you to bring to Canada, when you miss us just squeeze this soft dolphin" every inch of my nerves trembling in tension as I walk inside the airport to be far away from family for the first time is a scary new experience for me.

After a third time of security check finally calling for final boarding. "Philippine Airlines PR 2011 bound to Vancouver Canada is now ready for boarding". Slowly approaching my seat, the slow pace dropped to my chair. My heart dropped as the flight attendant announced "Mabuhay! And welcome to Philippine airlines, we are now departing Ninoy Aquino International Airport bound for Vancouver Canada." Uncontrollable tears started flowing as the plane took off up in the air.

Chapter 2

Canada
(2009)

feel like it was a suffocating sixteen hour flight. Among the four of us ladies got sponsored by this hospitality industry Claire is the quiet one while Jasmin and Angelica want to lead and make decisions. I'm not much of a talker when being around total strangers, we all get to know each other in Manila at the agency.

Stretching my legs limbering up, slowing pace rolling my carry-on luggage, heart thumping with excited eyes glowering around a massive mesmerizing International Vancouver airport. Brain flooding with questions of the unknown life I will be facing in this foreign Country. Head buzzing; muscles twitching; every step nearing the immigration office.

Crowded massive room with mixed ethnicity waiting for each turn for questions by an immigration officer. The four of us line up in one row of seating taking our documents out reviewing them once more. It's past four hours before we are all able to get out of the room then time to pick up our large luggage.

*For being first timers to be in a massive Vancouver international airport we were all well directed efficiently. Another waiting time at the arrivals area for Jessica to pick us up and bring us to our employers and hopefully to our staff housing. I have never missed a bed till this moment.

Slouching to my chair, four of us by the arrivals area, I snuggle into my brown coat closing my eyes "ladies just taking a power nap, please wake me up when Jessica arrives". It took twenty minutes for a tall curly golden blonde, blue-eyed woman walking towards our direction "I think that's her? She's the lady who interviewed us through skype. All four of us are unsure of who will pick us up.

Widely smiling "welcome to Canada ladies" shaking our hands introducing ourselves "pleasure to finally meet you Jessica," "Alpha, Jasmin, Angelica, and Claire, hope I say all your name right" "yes".

"I know you all must be tired from a long flight; we have about a three or four hours drive to go. Please feel comfortable sleeping in the car while we drive or enjoy the City of Vancouver". Talking while she walks us out the airport.

I step out the door a strong freezing ice air blowing to my face welcomes me in this frosty November weather. "I don't have a huge car were going to be a bit squishy, if you feel like needing a stretch, we can stop on the way please let me know". "Thank you, Jessica we appreciate your help," adjusting her side mirrors "thank you I'm glad you all made it here finally after long years of waiting" turning on the heater then turning the engine on.

Slowly going out in a busting cars traffic huge city people walking on the streets it's past four in the afternoon. Nothing seem different in my eyes as I watch from the car window all tall buildings, large offices, every full different cafe, large store of every designer brands you can think It feels like what I see in movies.

As we reached the sea-to-sky highway, a mesmerizing large open sea of water appeared. It's turquoise color glimmered, calling for us to jump in. The whole half hour drive allowed us to enjoy this wonderful view of nature. "Everyone hungry?" Jessica asked in a sleepy voice, with our tired voices we all answered together "yes!" we all laughed, having held our hunger for two hours. "Perfect!, I'm a bit starving too;we can stop at one of the best burger joints in town". We chowed down every bite polishing our plates and slurping cold soda. "Wow!, you ladies should have told me you were hungry; we could have stop earlier", I stood up stretching my leg and back. I said "it's ok Jessica; we know you traveled far to fetch us, so we thought we could wait." "We are almost there only about forty-five minutes and we arrived at our destination" we wrapped up then continued our journey.

I can feel the thrill of adventure as we entered a breathtaking winter wonderland with a large sign saying welcome to Whistler. I sat up straight in awe seeing the abundance of snow for the first time in my life; dreams and possibilities started unfolding as our journey went on.

We arrived at our destination and entered a lobby where Jessica welcomed us to wait. Across from where we seated, a front desk with one employee was engage in conversation with Jesicca. After ten minutes, Jesicca shared her inspiring words. "Ladies, it's an honor to meet you all. I will be returning home tomorrow, leaving you in the capable hands of your employer, who will guide you in settling into your new home". We all stood up, shaking her hands in gratitude. "Thank you for your invaluable assistance, we said. She beamed with bright smile, "You're all welcome. Embrace the opportunities Canada has to offer, ladies. Welcome to your new home, where your dreams will unfold.

With warmth and sincerity two visionary leaders, John and Carly greet us with open arms, their bright blue eyes sparkling with enthusiasm. As they introduce themselves I'm John, CEO of North lodging, and this is my siste and business partner Carly", as we rise shaking hands in gesture of mutual support. "My name is Alpha, huge thank you for sponsoring us to come here" I reply expressing my heartfelt gratitude for this transformative opportunity, as the other ladies rise up introducing and thanking both themselves "we are thrilled to have you all on board" John and Carly responded.

We toured every office and whole building. We step in a large office of the housekeeping department "this is where you will report every morning" leading us to one corner office table "meet your department manager Jose."

He stood up placing a document in his table briefly smiled "welcome ladies' pleasure to finally meet you all" two office tables form across Jose's "that's Phil and Joe our maintenance department" nodding their heads "hello".

Strolled to the hallway going back to the main lobby for a short briefing. Phil standing in front of the conference room arms crossed on his chest "so you're the new hire? From Philippines?" together in thrilled answered "yes!" he shivered and leaned back wards "welcome to hell ladies!" turns his back and walk away.

Twisting around staring at each other. Icy fear shooting to my brain, Jasmin glance to Angelica "what does he mean by that?" long moment of pause my pulse quickening. The door opened we all taken a back in surprise "the briefing is starting right now" we all gallop inside took a seat; the silence between us four continued till the briefing was over.

Its only five in the afternoon but it's already dark outside we settled in the room we are staying for the night hungry and exhausted "anyone wants to go out grab something to eat?" Claire hop out in bed "yes, I'm starving let's look around maybe restaurant is nearby" "yahhh let's explore were in Canada!" Angelica popping her head out from the washroom.

Icicle cascading lights flashing every street, huge, massive snow form like a volcano piled up in the middle of the village square. Every corner of the streets are busy people hands full of shopping bags. A large group of friends in their ski suits holding their skis on top of their shoulders ski poles hanging in their wrist all of them wearing a Santa hat walking inside a pub. All trees covered in snowflakes decorated with Christmas lights makes the whole place bright, jolly, and winter wonderland. We pass by a Korean restaurant a long golden light pine coned garland hang by the entrance door.

As we were enjoying eating our meal Jasmin waving up her fork with a fried tofu "I didn't realize it taste this delicious; if fried; all my life I only have this as a dessert" "yes, the softness reminds me of a sweet morning breakfast which me and my dad always awaits by our gate for the *taho peddler* to come by our house" sipping my coca cola while Angelica and Claire muttering under breath diving into their plates "I'm so sorry guys I'm starving" blubbering as she continued eating.

It was already nine thirty in the evening when we came back to the hotel. After taking a hot bath; I snuggled under the duvet. Lights are off and silence embracing the room pulling the duvet all way up to my head. I open my cellphone looking at my children's and family photos "*I'm thousands of miles away from my Country how much I'm missing my children and home.*" Turning my body sideways facing the wall *my* heart sank and a liquid of sadness flowing out my eyes.

The staff housing where we all live takes half hour to get to our workplace. Our one-week training as room attendants is tough. It's still dark and snowing heavily at five Friday morning. My foot feels so numb and tingly dragging myself out of the room stepping down the stairs towards the shower room with my eyes half open.

Jasmin is outside waiting for her turn to take shower "good morning" yawning stretching her arms up the air with a blue towel in her right hand "umagang kay ganda". I went straight down to the kitchen preparing breakfast and food to bring for lunch break. Angelica brewing some coffee while standing up by the kitchen counter Claire eating her bacon, egg, and rice. "Smells so good down here" pouring myself a cup of coffee "ohhh how much I miss nescafe maybe there's a Filipino store in town?" Angelica sipping her coffee "No not here in Pemberton, Gurlie said yesterday that only whistler has Filipino store, or we have to go to Vancouver if we want to stock up filipino food" "ohhh maybe we can plan sometime in our days off" glancing at the watch "oppss ladies half hour to go we need to catch our seventy thirty bus" like a flash we all pack, bundled up and head out the door.

Hopping in a comfortable relaxing tour bus is what I am amused most. I sat by the left window closing eyes for fifteen minutes and enjoy a five-minute fascinating scenery. One thing I'm fond of our half hour travel to whistler is looking out by the window enjoying a breathtaking view of green lake. When season changes this magical lake presents its own spectacular sight.

Mid week in November before the snow covers the water. The lake is calm and hard ice the tall mountain is all white and the snow sparkle like diamonds, the luxury million dolor homes from Nicklaus North reflects in the ice lake; feels like you're inside a snow globe. A million dollar experience you will keep coming back for more.

I can hear Claire snoring from across my seat. Ten minutes more and we arrived at the bus loop. The hotel where we work is just across from it. Wearing our lose collard red shirt pairing a yoga black pants and black shoes we all lined up in front of our managers table waiting for our tasks to be given by him. He sat quietly holding a bunch of folders his eyes gazing scrutinizing one by one of his ten room attendants.

We were teamed into four. Four of us are assigned at the outside properties. Many in these properties that our company managed are massive houses. Kenwoo drop us off in the snowsuit properties two huge units were given for us to clean.

Claire pulling the vacuum while Angelica carrying the cleaning tools. I am holding the front end of a heavy huge clear plastic bag full of clean white linens while Jasmin at the other end. I am carefully walking backwards leaving boot marks on a pack soft snow, every step towards the unit I can feel the numbness tingly palms radiating to my nerves and both my arms shaking as the load gets heavier with distance "this is what I don't like being assigned in this property this two massive units are too far from the parking area" Jasmin whining to herself.

Ken woo sprinting coming back from the unit passing by us "see you ladies in one hour we have more arrivals to clean after this" waving his hands goodbye; leaving us with his teasing smile.

Years ago, after earning my college diploma, I dream of being my own boss and running my own restaurant business.

But in this present moment, I am standing in front of bathroom sink full of slimy yellowish, sour rotten odor. Clipping my nose with my fingers turning the faucet on, in just few seconds the running water starts filling up the sink I swiftly turn the water off. Stepping out in the living room to breathe some air and then step back in the bathroom again.

With my eyes close, diving my right arm inside the sink, I felt the slimy particle crawling up to my skin as I grasp for the plug, quickly pulling it out. The rotten odor lingered in the bathroom as it drains, every inch of hair in my skin creeps as I quickly rinsing it off my arm. I immediately open the window sticking my head out blowing a huge exhale, sticking my nose took a whiff of the cold fresh snow falling, inhaling the fresh cold air; while staring at a beautiful tall pine tree all covered in white.

Dark started covering the clear blue skies it's past four thirty were all in a hurry to catch our five forty-five bus back to Pemberton, we can hear Ken woo calling on the radio but were all tied up to get our day done to answer. Angelica hauling a left and right hand full of heavy black garbage bag. I am in a hurry replenishing five housekeeping carts inside the storage. Jasmin coming back and forth in the storage bringing ten huge full clear bags of dirty linens. "What time is it? Are we going to make it on time for our bus?" Jasmin piling up the bags. "Maybe we can ask the houseman to finish clearing all this up they all know that that no more bus after five forty-five". Claire lining up four buckets full of damage kitchen utensils outside hallway beside the housekeeping storage room. "That last room we cleaned looks like got hit by a massive typhoon".

Not a word from each other walking towards the elevator. Every muscle in my body is aching. I took a deep breath. The elevator door opens and were surprised to see the face of the owner themselves. "Hello ladies we know your time is done but we need the last room clean, you will get paid overtime for two hours" Looking at each other in dismay "we will miss our bus and not another bus comes till nine thirty" "oohh no worries will have ken woo drive you ladies' home after" taps our back walking us back towards the housekeeping storage room "let's get it done ladies".

A moment of pause as I stood in the middle of two-bedroom suites that's three times a disaster in the last room we cleaned. I closed my eyes prayed in my head *dear lord give us more strength to finish our today and please help me and lead me to a better opportunity out there.*

So, this is spring. Birds chirping, snow melting, trees starts getting green, lakes starting to melt, flowers bloom and sun kissing to my skin. Light clothing is on.

Sat on a bench people passing by walking their dogs on their leashes. I can hear a streaming water running from behind. Inhaling deeply a fresh crisp air. Then I started to ponder, dreaming of running my own day care and having my mentally handicapped daughter helping me running it. This is Canada every opportunity is here I just need to start somewhere.

I step inside a tiny convenience store sliding the ice cream fridge open picking my favorite chocolate strawberry drumstick, I took the largest bag size of chili doritos walk towards the cashier. Her face look new in town but "hello how are you? Filipino?" smiling brightly "I'm good thanks, yes Filipino" Extending my hands "I'm Alpha, kumusta?" shaking my hands responding in her full of excitement tone of voice "I'm Rhea, so happy to meet a Filipino here I have only been here for two months" handing the items I bought " ohh welcome to Canada! Maybe we can hang out sometime" "yes! I would love that" "alright! See you around then" I wave goodbye head out the door.

We are holding a birthday party to one room mate in our staff housing. Jane is turning forty-eight she stood like a mother to all of us. Me and Rhea got assign to pick up the birthday cake ordered from Whistler. We took the early bus to be able to get back in time for the party.

Giji, Ronnie and Maya were assigned to cook another menu. While other house mates will cook their menu after work.

Afterpicking up the cake as we were walking towards our house I am catching for air can't breathe I can see the the smoke is too thick as we got nearer to our house, standing from across our staff housing squeezing through the crowds. Two fire trucks park in the entrance and back exit of the house.

Forcing myself to calm down seeing thick heavy grey smoke coming out from the windows. "ohh my God my passport and documents" my heart skipping a beat "ohhh nohh our house is on fire!" panic zipping through her body.

Two firemen holding a fire extinguisher coming out the entrance door stepping down the stairs. "it's all good everyone there is no fire, smoke are coming from the burnt four chicken that has been left inside the oven, it's all safe now" blowing a huge air from my nose in relief "thank God" turning to Rhea "I guess we can get in the house now" squeezing through the space of a crowded neighbors "excuse us please, excuse us" Rhea extending both arm up holding the birthday cake forcing between spaces the jam pack of people crowding our front yard.

We storm inside a disaster mudroom. Giji wiping large dripping windows dry. Ronnie clearing the full kitchen and prepping for another menu "everyone ok? what happen you guys?" stepping closer towards the kitchen my socks soaking wet from the sprinting water coming out from the carpet "the thick smoke triggered the fire sprinklers that's why carpet is wet it looks like raining inside here a while ago" "what cause the smoke?" Ronnie sipping his soda "we left four chicken cooking in the oven then we realize we need few ingredients we left and went to the store which we thought will make it on time to get back, unfortunately leaving four chickens unattended can be dangerous". Jane interrupted who is wiping the furniture dry "alright everybody should we cancel the party? Or what you guys think with all this mess?" we all look at each other "yes! party must go on".

We heard the fire truck wailing away. I took a deep breath and went downstairs to clean the clutters before visitors come rushing in for the party. I Heard someone knocking by the door. A tall Caucasian man with blue eyes stood smiling widely "hi my name is James" extending his hands "ohh hi Alpha, how can I help?" peaking his head inside the house "I was one of the volunteer firefighters helping earlier thought just to check on you guys if any help you need" "yeah come in come in don't take your shoes off the whole carpet is wet" leading him up the stairs.

"Nay! Someone's here to help" extending his arm introducing himself to everyone "hello I'm James's I'm an electrician if you need any help in your house please gave me a call" handing his business card to each one "thank you" Jane came closer asking questions "thank you for offering your help we need someone to fix our stairway" "I was going to say yeah no problem I can come by tomorrow I don't have my tools I live by two blocks from here I will come after work tomorrow" Jane shaking his hands endlessly "thank you! Thank you, why don't you stay join us tonight for dinner it's my birthday" "ohh thank you I didn't bring anything ok ill come back later at what time?" "it's at six tonight" "ok ill come back tonight then thank you, and happy birthday".

Table is a feast; every Filipino special dish is served in the table. Guest started coming in it is getting crowded and loud in the living room. I went up to my room open my laptop and connected my magic jack dialed the number back home phone rings twice and my daughter's voice I heard "hello" her innocent sweet voice most beautiful to hear in my ear "hi anak how are you, where is your kuya?" "Hello, mom! kuya is upstairs" "how are you langga?"

I can hear footsteps running down the stairs "ohh here's kuya mom" tears start flowing "I miss you both so much" "hi mommy! How are you" my son's voice echoing in my ears "we miss you mom" my heart sank as I hear both my children very happy and teasing each other "mommy thank you for the roller blades I really have fun with it, but grandma only let's me play in the weekend" wiping my tears dry "lannga please listen to grandma ang help her look after your sister ok, I love you both and miss you both so much".

Sat in my bed tears kept flowing the longing to be with them feels like my heart going to explode. The sound of silly laughs and teasing jokes when family get together every Sundays. And here I was working a job I couldn't imagine I would do, worst part is to have a cruel boss. Maybe I don't belong here in Canada; must not be for me. I sat and prayed and question him above. What is the purpose why brought me in this place? To be with people I don't even know if I can trust. Staying miles away from my children and family is worth the sacrifice? This longingness I can't stand. Took my pack of cigarettes from the side drawer run down the stairs passing by the living room loud drunken people singing in bad tones zipping my winter coat closing the sliding door behind me lighting a cigarette my red swollen eyes feels relieve from the touch of cold air. Standing there in silence and started dreaming of the career and life I wanted to achieve. I heard the sliding door opened but did not bother to look back who it was.

"You miss the party" a familiar man's voice walking closer to my end he stood beside me I turn my head and as suspected it's James handing me a bottle of corona "hello glad you came and you seem to be having a good time at the party" "it's my first time being at a Filipino gathering" blowing smoke away "ohh yeah, how did you like our food?" "it's good very tasty, you guys cook enough for the whole neighbours" hilariously laughing at his statement "it's a huge feast indeed" his stepping closer towards me "I walk my dog every morning I notice you ladies walking out catching the bus, where do you work?"

"I work as a room attendant in one of the property managements in Whistler, what about you James?" sips his beer flirty smiled "I work as an electrician in school district" turning to face him "ohh great I assume you have been in the company for many years now?" "yeah I want to stay for the good benefits for my daughter" "how many kids you have?" "I only have one" nodding my head "me I have two, and its driving me crazy being thousands of miles away from them" staring out in the clear stary night "you can bring them here ya'h know" chugs his beer "I don't know if I belong in this type of world or life I have a different dream" taking the empty beer bottle safely putting it by the corner "I will just finish my contract and take it as a great experience" "your children will have a better future here" sounding convincing "my situation is different cause my daughter has special needs she's mentally handicapped I don't know how to make it work taking care of her and working at the same time" we sat by the dinning area I opened another bottle beer for myself and for him "you know there is a lot of support here for your daughter" "is that so?" with a puzzled face he continued talking about opportunities in Canada. "Sounds very uplifting thank you for the info" "thank you for having me I guess I have to go my daughter is sick at home but she is ok by herself she's ten" "ohhh of course thank you for coming" he stood and kiss the back palm of my hand, surprise by his unexpected gestures but I smiled; and nod; swifty taking my hands off.

"I will see you tomorrow ill come after work to fix your stairs have a goodnight." "Have a goodnight" waving goodbye watching him leave out the door.

I drop myself in bed hang my leg against the wall, my feet is killing me and my whole body is aching after a long hard day at work close my eyes to relax for a moment thanking God for surviving a stressful and challenging day. Few minutes later I hear someone knocking on the door "yes come in" Jane peaking her head from the door "hi Nay, come in" finishing her fish style hair down to her waist "Alpha, James is downstairs to fix our stairs I have a feeling he likes you can you go down to check if he needs anything maybe we can get discount on the job he is going to do" dragging myself out the bed "Nay I can go check but you know I just had a bad break up from my boyfriend back home" "yes, I know but just go see him I know his more of after seeing you than fixing the stairs" rolling my eyes "alright! Alright! But Nay! Stop assuming things" teasingly laughing.

I did not bother changing my shorts and tank top putting a white cover up brushing my hair with my fingers running downstairs out the door. "Hi James, how are you today? Anything I can help you with?" taking out his tools from his white working van "no, it's ok it's not going to be long" nailing out the broken wooden stair then measuring the new replacement. "So, how did your day go today?" I sat at the top of the stairs while his nailing the new replacement "nothing out of ordinary just work" "yeah same here, can I offer you anything to drink?" "maybe later thank you" inhaled deeply before asking the question "by the way James, Nanay is asking if how much will your service cost" smiling brightly as he finish the work "I will talk to her" "ok, sounds good thank you again for the help" cleaning up all his tools back to his van and we went inside "nay James wants to talk to you" turning the stove down facing James "here have some beer thank you for your help" Jane handing him the bottle "thanks" immediately sipping his beer "Nay, since you stand as the mother in this house instead of paying me can I ask Alpha for a dinner date tonight instead?" my hips sway around from the kitchen table trembling voice "sorry did I hear it right?" James's step closer to where I was shocked standing "if your Nanay will allow me to take you out for a date will you come have dinner with me please?" tingling starts crawling up from my belly strikes to my thumping heart glace a stare to Jane raising my eyebrows and she made a signal by her hand to go, there I was being a good house mate "aahhh yes ok is it tonight?" James happily smiled "yes, ill pick you up at seven tonight and thank you for coming with me" kissing at the back of my palm and went on his way out "see you tonight then" as I wave goodbye.

James made a huge impression for a first date, though I'm not ready to date yet after coming from a painful break up, but I need to be a helpful house mate. A fancy and popular high-end restaurant in town I have been wanting to experience since migrating in Canada.

We tossed, as the red wine reaches my tongue it's bold rich flavors of blackberry the full body taste captures the essence of its intensity just perfect to my liking. "woow I love this wine" "yes they only serve the best in here enjoy" James placing the black napkin to his lap "so you know how to cook?" hilariously laughing with his question "I don't claim to be an expert but I sure can cook" smiling brightly "that's good enough, cheers" clanking our wine glasses.

Chapter 3

///

Life as a Filipino Immigrant

Growing up from a tropical country like Philippines life is a huge turn around change from the cold weather to the range of different ethnicity and social backgrounds, career and all else this country brings great opportunity.

Warm sunny day on Tuesday morning. I'm wearing a white bathing suit topping it with a haltered boho black and white striped. James came in the door "hi are you ready?" full of smiles taking my beach bag "bring water bottle with you; it's too warm out there" "oohh right" slid off to the kitchen took my water bottle from the freezer then large chips from the cupboard, slipping on my black adidas flip flops and out to his white van.

Brings out his charm wearing light yellow short pairing with a red collar shirt showing off his pinkish toes with his white Nike slip on with his manly black sunglasses. "Have you done kayaking in the lake before?" glancing towards the driver's seat brushing my hair with my fingers "no, I haven't really had any chance I just want to rest when I get days off work mostly or go to Vancouver do a shoe shopping" laughing with my statement "I hate the traffic in the city but if your going next time let me know Ill drive you" "ohh that's really thoughtful thanks ill keep that in mind".

Water bottles, chips, and a six pack of kokanee beer and paddles piling it all up in the middle of the kayak we both slide it in the lake. Surrounded with large mountains and the clear blue skies touching the turquoise water feels like heaven. One lady passing us by going back to shore in her blue paddle board, young children diving from the middle dock, a group of five men in the speed boat round and round screaming joyfully while others hanging by the beach relaxing reading books or playing some card games. "Wooww I love beach and I have been to a few beach resorts back home but I have never seen this kind of majestic place" James opening a can of beer we sat facing each other at the ends of the kayak "welcome to Canada! this is what we do on our leisure time so enjoy we only have two months of summer here" cheers! "Thank you, James, glad I came".

Were floating away in this majestic paradise I laid back relax closing my eyes taking advantage of the warmth of the sun kissing through my whole body.

To be in a country where I am not accustomed to, I find every lifestyle totally odd as James paddled, I let my frustrations, misery, stress, pain, and longingness float away down in the deep waters feed it to every organisms down in the bottom and never let it come ashore.

Many friends I know from back home still dreaming and working hard to come to Canada, but chance is too harsh for them. But here I was given a huge opportunity that thousands of people dream to have.

The long moment of silence got interrupted when James ask me unexpected question. "Why move to Canada?" I sit up straight and started paddling "well, aside from wanting to experience I made a tough decision for my children's future" sipping my warm beer as I continue to tell my story "It's unfortunate that father of my children is able to walk away from his obligations which lead me no choice but to work hard to provide for my children it's one saddest painful reality in our Country we cannot run after the father of our kids".

We end our day with a blast reclining the passengers seat wrapping my wet hair with towel. After fifteen minutes drive my eyes starts to close, I feel like my whole energy suck up by the sun the peace and tranquility of James driving feels like a cradle.

The long one-hour drive felt short I woke up when James's parking his van. The van stop in front of unrecognizable home "where are we?" asking James still half asleep "this is my house let's have dinner no worries I'll cook then ill walk you home" "ohh ok thank you" opening the car door holding my hand as I step out the van.

James went straight to the kitchen taking out stuff from his fridge "hope it's ok I don't eat much rice?" "ohh yes no problem at all as long as it's not seafood" "it'll be quick" turning the stove top heating up the pan.

"James hope you don't mind can I smoke out at the deck" he walks towards the living area sliding the door open towards the deck "I don't have astray I don't smoke so here" passing me an empty can of beer I lighted my cigarette James walk back in I sat in a garden chair sun is still up at seventy thirty in the evening I can feel the heat from his back deck large pine tress lining up from his house all the way to the end of his neighbors. James's dog named baby sat in the grass calm but alert for bears coming and going in his backyard.

The round dinning table looks festive a center piece of red candlelight, a red bottle of wine. Fried shrimp with a spinach dip for appetizer, Caesar salad, a delicious prime rib for main course and pumpkin pie with vanilla ice cream on top for dessert. "ohhh wooww I'm so full and you're a great cook" sipping my second glass of red wine "sshhh, don't tell anyone I can cook" winking his eye jokingly laughs at his own joke. I put the left overs in separate Tupperware's, took the dirty glasses and plates and cutleries from the wood round table placing them all at the kitchen sink while James started washing dishes by hand "I don't use dishwasher I find it too waste of water and electricity" drying the cleaned dishes putting it aside by the counter "I don't know where goes where and yes I totally agree with you about the dishwasher" I check my watch and it's nine thirty already "wowww day went by quickly, thank you for a wonderful day James and for the tasty dinner I had a great time" "welcome" gently pulling my right arm wrapping his strong arms around my waist with my chest closer to his then mouth meets mine. It took a few seconds after I realized and puling away from him with a thumping heart like a drum "ohh ahh sorry I did not expect that, have goodnight, James ill call you tomorrow" "ill walk you home I need to walk my dog too" grabbing all my stuff in the mud room and his putting his boots on "ohh ok yeah yeah sure".

Today I'm working alone all day in one property. All are arrivals, among the check out rooms five are two-bedroom suites and three are single bedroom, then I have five stayovers to do. I find doing thirteen rooms for one day seem a lot for one employee, but I don't have a choice. Being tied in a contract with the company all I can do is to face every demanding work that is given to me day by day.

Pushing a loaded heavy housekeeping cart in the hallway to do my next two bedroom check out room when a vision of myself running a home daycare and my daughter will be there to help me with the children ill be looking after a simple dream that one day will be realized.

Turning my cart around blocking the entrance. Holding a large black garbage bag in my hand standing in distress my mouth drop staring at the state of the kitchen, strips of greasy bacon hanging from the pan the grease splatter all over the stove top, kitchen counter full of sticky pasta sauce every dinner plates empty bottles of liquors laying from the counter to down the kitchen floor, empty beer cans scattered from kitchen to the living room all the way to both bedrooms, bathroom towels hanging every fixtures in the room my mind running like thunderbolt seeing the state of this room being turn upside down. *"ohhh this is going to take me a long time to clean by myself".* I glance in my watch I still have two more rooms to do and its two thirty in the afternoon arrival rooms need to get done by four. I dialed the manager's office "hello Jose, I just want to let you know that the room I'm doing right now is too dirty and will take me longer than usual to clean it and I still have two more room to clean I will be needing help" I can hear him from the line exhaling deeply " I will try to send you help, everybody is busy finishing their work if no one will come for you by three you need to finish it by yourself" "but I need to catch my bus or else I will be stuck here in village till nine forty five for the last trip" "your bus is not my problem I just need you to finish the room stay longer if u must just get it all done" the line was immediately cut. Rushing to finish cleaning my anxiety shrinking in "I can't believe I just heard that from a boos mouth". Guess this is reality being a contract worker in Canada you get sh*t! And abused!

It's pass six in the evening I pass by the front desk "hey Alpha?! You just finish?" lifting my shoulders inhaling deep "yeah" rolling her eyes "you know I suggest to file complaint to your jerk boss, that's why no room attendants lasts because of his abusive ruling" "thanks Tia but I don't think I have that option being on contract" I felt her being sad "anyway ill see you when I see you; have a good shift" I wave goodbye and out the dark cold night crossing towards the bus stop thinking in my head what to do for three hours wait till the last trip bus back home.

I took a pink cap I have spent lots of money in my face need to protect it from the heat of the sun. Wearing my Merrel brown hiking boots jeans shorts and black crisscross sports top. With a water bottle in hand James have been waiting outside sitting by the bottom stairs facing the sun. Looking amazing wearing a black ryder sunglasses and a red cap "ok ready when you are" jumping down the stairs he instantly stood up touching his lips to my face "ok let's go there a trail we can start hiking just across here" leading me at the front neighbors leads to a back trail.

"I used to hike with my brother and group of friends back home, there's only one popular mountain called mt. agad-gad" "how long will it get you to the top?" stirring up James curiosity "about four hours or more depends who your with" laughing together with my last statement "this hike will go today is not difficult but you will enjoy the scenery as we go along" "ohh really I'm excited! I don't do nothing on my days off aside sleeping in and facing my laptop talking to my children and family home".

Dry trail dust starting to accumulate in my boots its has been half hour since we started hiking and we have not reached the bottom trail of Nairn Falls. We decided to take a break sat on a huge rock sip some water and had a sandwich James made " wow I didn't think of bringing some food with me all I know when we hike alcohol is what we bring hahaha" James choking from his sandwich laughing hard "well, good thing I have some beer for us to drink when we get to the top" joyful wide eyes tapping him at his shoulders "that's awesome!" finished our sandwich and continued our journey.

Another half hour later I can hear strong current of water getting louder and louder as we get nearer and nearer. I can feel the cold mist in the air walking fast as I am getting to anxious to see these popular Nairn Falls. "We are here at the top of the falls" opening his arm wide out in the air we are both looking down the unceasing strong flowing turquoise water hikers taking selfies and other group of hikers even went down near to take photos it's a one busy mountain popular to many hikers some are here for the first time like me and some and coming back to enjoy its natural beauty.

My brain starts buzzing as we reached the astounding view at the top. We sat in the middle under a shade of a small pine tree. I paused in silence listening to the loud strong current water falls streaming, leaning my back on the pine tree closing my eyes I never felt so relax after hours of hiking and took a quick nap.

After a meeting with an immigration consultant from one of the local cafés I am thrilled with the positive news about my residency application. I went straight home to call my children and family about the wonderful news.

Stepping up the stairs I can hear voices of arguments coming from the dinning area. Sounds like I'm coming home with room mates in chaos. Taking my shoes off Jane voice is calm and settle explaining about some issues, Jasmin voice of tone is shaking and raising towards Jane "wait, wait Jas you're not listening" I am coming in quietly tiptoeing walking up the stairs everyone gathering by the dinning area voicing out concerns and other matters towards Jas. This is not what I expect to come home to; of all days why it needs to be today.

Jane catch me in her eye "Alpha! Stop, come over here we want everyone to open up we all live in same house we can all at least open to one another if any complains or concerns and as a mother in the house I want us all to treat each other like family here" I turn around down the stairs and stride towards the window "I am not sure what's going on nay but I'll listen" Jas fierce red teary eye glared at me "is she also involved in this!?" every muscles of her finger shaking pointing towards me "she's not even at home mostly!! more often going out with her man!" Jane calmly holding her hands "calm down we are not looking for a fight here we want to settle everybody's issue in the house, we can talk in civilized manner ok" Jas bursting in tears "why all of you are ganging up on me?!, this woman here shouldn't be getting involved in here!" again pointing to my direction and I just stood in silence watching Jas and the rest of the ladies in confusion without any clue what the commotion is all about. I did not realize that Jas seem to have issue against me keeps pointing to my face with full of hateful eyes not having any clue, because I am not sure if I have offended anyone in the house if I did, I am sorry I don't know. For forty five minutes stood quietly while Jane settle and fix everyone issues. We all disperse and went inside our perspective room.

Claire started her tablet, and I started my laptop. Ever since we are in same room we rarely talk or open to each other. She set her boundaries since we became room mates. We sat in each other's twin bed in silence logging in to my Facebook account it's been a while since the last time I check. Raining message through and through from family, colleagues, and friends all has same questions how to apply to come to Canada.

After a wonderful conversation with my children and family, while waiting for my laptop to shutdown Claire move an inch facing me "so, you want to get stuck with this company?" unexpected question I never thought for myself "hmmm, I am really having a hard time with the job we do, I mean the job itself is not a problem it's the people were working with, particularly with a full on discrimination from your own boss" "that's exactly how I feel also" Claire blurted out with huge regret drawn in her face "I don't think I can stay anymore longer here" as I close my laptop putting it away inside my luggage underneath my bed "I totally know how your feeling Claire but we don't have a choice we signed a contract with this company". Raising her eyebrows laid down in bed turning her back away from me "goodnight, Claire let's keep praying this shall pass, many families from our country dream of being here but never given a slight chance, but for us we are given a huge opportunity being here let's make the most of it". Claire just inhaled deep and no words.

(-The loud clanking of cutleries and plate down from the kitchen waken me up. I can sense the tension of their conversation. A blasting knocking on my door "Alpha! Wake up!" Jane blowing the door wide open "what's going on Nay?" stormed towards Claires closet "Claire is gone!?" still half awake "you mean gone went to work Nay?" an empty closet and clothing drawers Jane flip Claires bed linen both her two large luggage's are gone. "ohhh nohhh did she run away Jane?" the rest of the ladies barging in the room one by one. "This is going to be so bad for us" Angelica stated in her worried tone "I hope this is not going to affect our application for residency" we all stay still for a moment absorbing to what mess Claire has left for all of us. "We need to report this to the agency, right?" looking at Jane "I will email but let's pray and hope that it will not affect us badly".

That night when all of us are home from work. We sat in the dinning table pass the laptop around for us to read the email came from the agency. Claire was last seen caught in camera in one of the buses going Kelowna and that she was reported to the immigration and are on a hunt for her to be deported. We all eat our supper in silence worried of what will happen to Claire and what will the mess she left will reflect to all of us.

Afraid of what will the outcome of what Claire has done. I refrained myself in trusting anyone I'm around with. Keeping my unknown future to myself. I stood waited for the bus it's unusual it's late. I find it peaceful and safe hanging at the public library calling them through skype I can open to my family and speak to my children freely without any hesitations.

"Why don't you come home for a short visit so you can take a break from your miseries" hearing from my dad a man with few words felt like an arrow striking my heart hundred times. "How I wish it's that simple Dad, but I'm not sure if I am allowed with my application for residency still on going". "Maybe there is a way" I smiled "I will look into it dad".

I get too overwhelmed with the responsibilities that is put on my shoulder and being tied in contract with one company I need to be careful at my work and people I am surround with. I always look forward to biweekly Fridays when paycheck comes in after rent is taken out from our paycheck there isn't much left for extra to save. When sending money home for my children's tuition fee, dad medicine, budget for their groceries and more basic needs there is only much left for myself and always end up on a tight budget. I am financially frustrated but I have a strong fate and believed that God has his reasons for my struggles that one day things will turn around.

Warm sun everyone in town loves to be out in the sun. The water park is a nice pace to hang around seeing children having fun in water slides, water tubes, playing with their beach sand toys. I laid my towel in the grass put some sunscreen on wearing my huge beach hat to cover my face laid in the towel and started turn the page on the last chapter of Danielle Steel new release novel I could hardly put it down.

I move to a near by huge tree to get some shade perfect spot while I wait for James to come after his work the sun is getting too hot burning into my skin. I was about to close my eyes to take a nap when a loud cries of a young five-year-old boy screeching to my ears "what did I told you!?" a dad with huge body build yelling and vigorously slapping the back of the hand of an innocent child. A kind of discipline I despise in my growing years as a child.

Memories flashing vividly inmy head as I hear the loud cries of the five-year-old boy, his dad scolding him and slapping the child repeatedly on the palm.

My mind brought me back when the time when I was ten years old, emotionally distress with all the things going on in my life. I was a menace and kept running into trouble during my childhood days. My mom loves to collect chinawares, and because her collections are expensive, she keeps all of them in a nice glass display case in our living room. I couldnt help but find all of her collections so pretty and want to play with them. So, what I did was called four of my friends to come and play with me at home, and I took every china ware my mom displayed. We were all having too much fun; my friends accidentally broke half a dozen of my mom small plates. I was terrified. I sent all my friends home and taped together every plat, putting them back in the display glass case. That night after my mom came home, she pass by the display case; her eyes widened in fear. "what happened to my beautiful china plates!" loud voice echoing every corner in the living room. Dad; sprinted out the bedroom towards where my mother standing. I hid in the corner of the dinning table frighteningly sweating. My dad started calling our names one by one, we lined up straight in front of our parents." The three of us looking at each other, as my dad asked "who was playing with this?" pointing to every broken valuable pieces. The three of us were quiet. And I was so afraid to admit it. "No one speaks?! all of you will be punished" my father roared. Then my sister spoke up, "I saw you playing with it and your friends this afternoon" pointing to me. Scared to face my mothers anger, I hid behind my brothers back. "You!" my mother pointed towards me. "Go! and kneel in front of the altar! stay there until I say so!; reflect on what you've done". And I kneeled in tears.

After a short-day work, I went to my boss office to follow up with the paperwork that my lawyer is waiting for my employers to sign. Jose is talking on phone when I came in so, I sat in the chair beside his working table waiting. While I sat and waited for half an hour, I visioned reaching my dream when my permanent residency is approved, having my two children over here and running my own child day care center along with my daughter helping me with the kids. In God's perfect time it will happen.

Jose finally done talking on the phone "yes what can I do for you?" I stood up stepping closer to his table "I want to get the paperwork from my lawyer that needed signature for my residency application?" slightly nod "ohhh that yes, yes, I'm sorry I did not get the chance to have it signed yet come back tomorrow I will see them first thing in the morning" rolling my shoulders with the disappointment this has been the third time I followed up and get the same answer every time it keeps delaying and delaying with my application.

After exiting the building, I pace myself towards the ice cream house. The line up is all way out to the bridge I stood at the end of the line my mind floating away for my application and tons of paperwork pending. This whole process is going to be a long journey. I sat at the bench with my mint flavor ice cream on cone indulging my disappointment away with the delicious, sweet taste.

My cellphone ring and it's James's calling "hey, how's it going?" I can hear a wind blowing through his phone "I'm still driving where are you at?" licking my ice cream "I'm near by the cows Ice cream" "ok stay there I'll be there in ten minutes" "ok sure, see you soon, bye".

James came after fifteen minutes in a hurry "come on let's go" "what's going on where are we going?" reached for my hand locking his fingers to mine "we better hurry the concert just started and it's a really great band that's playing tonight" "ohh I don't have any idea there is a concert going on, how much is the ticket?" "it's free let's hurry before we can't get any spot to sit" "ohh wow I've never been to free concerts" were walking fast I can hear the band playing as we get nearer and it's an outside concert by the plaza.

Huge crowd everyone bringing their own chair to sit on some sat on the grass others laid blankets or towels "this is super cool" James laid a blue blanket together we sat side by side he opened a can of cider poured in a plastic cup one for him one for me "cheers!" it's seven thirty in the evening and the sun still high up the massive crowd having a blast with the band playing.

The concert finished at nine thirty in the evening the darkness just started crawling in. "I parked at lot four there's a short cut over here" we walk towards the back plaza crossing towards the parking area one by one cars started to disperse in the parking lot and were still walking around looking for which spot he parked too much in hurry to watch the concert he forgot which spot he left his car. "hahahhaa, your funny but cute James I can't believe at your age you can be a little reckless but its cute" winking and teasing at him "well at least you find me cute than being annoyed by it" "alright, alright let's focus on finding your car" were laughing as we continue searching around the area.

Arriving to Canada with no clue what life will be there for me is one terrifying thought keeps crossing in my mind. I remember during the time when my grandmother Linda Sabayle was still alive, I use to tell her what I picture of myself becoming in my future career. "Lola, I'm going to be a flight attendant, travelling many places around the globe, meet and learn different people, and then when I have saved money, I want to bring Mom and Dad travelling with me" The vision of myself being flight attendant felt sure real whenever I'm telling my grandma about it. Then my Lola will have me sit beside her "look child my lovely apo there is nothing wrong with your dreams, but I would suggest to change your career being flight attendant is like your digging half of your grave once plane crashes there is slim chance of survival" shrugging my shoulder "do you always have to say that all the time Lola?" she holds my hand and says "I don't want to lose a beautiful apo, your bound to better life and career I can see that in you" smiling brightly "thank you Lola, love you to the max".

But now here I was stuck to a company where discrimination is at it's best and a job, I take pride to is being look down by many. But I have a strong will of changing my path.

At five forty-five I'm sitting at the table so full of hope waiting for the class to begin at six thirty. Minutes later, few students starts coming in that the room starts to fill. Early childhood education is an expensive field to take so I want to make sure of it that I'm not missing one class. For the next six months three times a week for four hours every class will be a long full of adventures.

I have been looking forward for this week's days off. I printed posters since last week. I took the seven-morning bus to make a productive day. First place I have in mind to post my marketing flyer is at the public library. One of the customer service representatives giving me her warm welcoming smile as I step inside the building, I immediately approach her extending my hand Introducing myself "hi how are you today" shaking hands "I'm great thanks how can I help you?" I stated my affair "is there any chance I can post a flyer in here?" handing her my marketing flyers "ohhh flyers like this can be posted in any community build board in town" "I see thank you for the help". The day went by fast walking around posting flyers wherever I can possibly post. It's past five and need to catch my bus home. Leaning against a wall pinching my leg down to my calf a shooting pain after all the running and walking all day posting my flyers. I hope to get even just one client from all the posters.

Just in time I sat in the bus it started pouring heavily outside. Every time when weather like this reminds of what my dad use to tell me that when it rains that's the heaven pouring blessings upon us. And when a rainbow appears after the rain you can make one wish and it will be granted. But I wonder myself if the heavens does listens to any of my prayers and wish. As I think and look back from my past, *I believe I was in grade three back then we have been sitting in the study area for hours staring at the same page of the book with endlessly tears and snout nose. Her fingers pointing to a green mango drawn in the page yelling with same question for the tenth time "is this sweet!, sour! or salty?!" sweating palms, quivering bleeding lips, cringing from my chair, as she asked the same question once again "it's salty" answered in shivering tone, with a high speed the book splattered to my face left my skin burning hot and numb "still wrong answer! we've been discussing this for hours and your answer still wrong!" she grabs my hair banging my head to the table "your so dumb! You're never going to succeed in life!" pointing her sharp nails to my face "pray that God will give you better future with your small squirrel brain only the heavens can help you to better your life!! because I will not take care a stupid dumb child like you all my life!" I started organizing my schoolbooks vigorously whipping "get up to your room and think all what you have learn for tonight!". Heavy heart stepping every staircase.*

I snap from my thoughts as the bus driver hits the brake hard. I got thrown from my seat a massive deer crossing the street almost got hit by the bus. I was going to take a quick video I've never seen such massive deer all my life, but it quickly disappeared in the bushes.

I step out the bus puddles of water splashing under my boots a gasoline station near by to get some roof till the rain slows down. As I reached a trail I stop and stood still a moment of pause unzip my jacket turning my face up towards the sky catching every rain drops to my face. I close my eyes open my arms wide taking every plop of rain to my face and made a wish and said a prayer as the water rain dribbles to my skin. Turning around in circles soaking in the rain with a joyful heart I thank the heavens for all the blessings bestowed upon me.

Tiptoeing coming in the house liquid dripping through my pants quickly slid inside the bathroom took my clothes off squeezing the water. Tying my pink bathrobe rush to the laundry room took my other dirty clothes started the washer. Jasmin leaning by the wall staring at what I'm doing with arm crossing on her chest "where have you been? Always out on your date with James again?" I sense her irritable tone "I have business to attend to why?" raising her eyebrows "you seriously forget that it's your schedule to do the house cleaning today?" smacking my forehead with my palm "ohhh nohh I totally forgot! Ok ill start cleaning right now" I dash to the storage grab all the cleaning supplies and rapidly started cleaning the washrooms. Jasmin stood by the stairs glaring at me till I finished cleaning the first bathroom "yes, anything else?" she turns around walk away without a single word.

The long rectangular table is full for an early breakfast. There's eight of us sitting together joyful and loud. Everyone can't keep the excitement our moving day to Whistler after almost two years of searching a place for all of us to be in one house we finally found a place where bus is running every thirty minutes and nearer to our workplace, unlike Pemberton only four schedule of bus running in a day difficult for someone like us who is afraid to drive especially in winter season.

Chapter 4

///

A Hopeful Heart

Six months after moving to our new home the place is tinier than our previous one. But, we feel lucky to be able to get a place temporarily in this expensive town. To live and getting a place to rent is hard to get. It's a bungalow house situated in the middle of massive pine trees a wide-open lawn in the front. luckyly Jane is able to get a place to rent in this touristy town with affordable amount where all homes are over a million of dollars that ordinary employees like us will never be able to afford to own one.

Since our moving to Whistler James always picks me up after work, he never fails to bring either box of chocolate or bouquet of flowers. In times when an unforeseen circumstance happens in the highway, he always finds a way to be on time to wait for me when I finish working. As soon as he sees me coming out the door, he gets out from his car to open the passenger door for me; always takes my heavy working bag; putting them at the back sit. Every time when were together James always makes me feel like a precious jewel, but even then I am hesitant trusting him fully.

looking back from early *last year. I was engaged to a man I thought I will be sharing my forever with. I was on the phone talking to my dad. "What documents needed dad for our wedding?" I can hear from the other line my father holding a paper and pen "ok so this is what we need from Jake, certificate of no marriage and his birth certificate and same goes for you but with yours I can obtain those documents; I will just need an authorization letter from you" with a ceasing smile my heart is full of joy; "thank you for the help dad, I'll give Jake a call" ; "ok, tell him to drop the documents over ill take care of the rest"; "amazing dad, love you dad! talk soon".*

As soon I put down the call, I dialed Jake "hey how are you?" "hi sweetheart I miss you I'm still on a meeting but your more important than work" "hmmm really?," my way of teasing him "so by the way dad is asking for our wedding preparations when I get back this November documents we need to provide like certificate of no marriage and your birth certificate" a long sight and silence on his line "hello Jake? Sweety are you still there?" I heard a door shutting from Jakes end of the line "sweetheart I need to tell you something, but please keep in my mind I love you and your important in my life" biting my lip my mind started to wander of what his about to say "I can't provide a certificate of no marriage because I was married before but that was over long time ago even before I met you, she is now in states I have no communication with her for a long time" silent tears rolling on my cheek my heart suddenly felt weak "for four years you never told me this!? You lied to me all these years!? I trusted you?!" I never gave him a chance to speak I immediately cut the line turn my phone off cover myself under the duvet whipping till I fall asleep.

I glance at James eyes twinkling while focus on the road listening to his favorite local radio station sharing about his day at work. He drove slowly as we pass green lake "look at that such a beautiful place to live" looking out the window and the turquoise color of lake reflected in my eyes "yes, it is" he then drove in normal speed "I feel lucky to be here, but I feel lonely until I met you" I pause for a moment listen to my heart not sure how to respond to his statement.

We sat in one round table waiter serving a welcome champagne the club is jam pack. Elizabeth been dancing for hours by the stage she's on a holiday visa from Australia and since arriving to Canada she loves to party at night and skiing by day. Working when she feels like it. Sam bought a round of tequila shots for the whole gang "one, two, three shot!" the five of us chug the shotglass "whhoowhh dude! that was smooth." Kitty swaying her arms up the air, and I love listening to her British accent. The DJ went up the stage with a megaphone announcing, "are you ready to partyyyy!!" the crowd went wild, we all jump out our table and hit the dance floor.

"Heyy Alpha!" Abby yelling at me from our table in her wobbly tone "yerrr phone don't stop ringing" sprinting from the dance floor my nose suddenly got a whiff of a crunchy tortilla, with melted cheese and pickled jalapeno made my stomach grumbling "ohhh the delicious smell of the nachos made me feel starving" taking my cellphone from Abby's hand "thanks Abby I need to answer this" cram myself to the congested dance floor looking for a quieter spot to answer the phone there was a fifteen miss calls from James.

"Helloo Jamess!" I can hardly hear him on the line swooping in the washroom "hey how's it going?" "Great clubbing with friends" "I can hear that; I was in town meeting a friend at the pub I can drive you home if you want?" I check my watch it's pass one in the morning "ohhh I think that's a good idea I had few drinks already." "Ok sounds good I'm already park outside" "ohh you know which club I am?" "Yeah, Jane told me I been calling, and you did not answer so I ask her I will wait for here I can't leave the car". I grab my purse "I have to go guys James is outside picking me up thank you for the fun time guys" "what? The party not over yet he always does that since you're dating him" Jess now sober from dancing "there is always a next time Jess" slid my leather jacket on "wait, here is to a last shot for crazy night" Sam handing me a last shot of Jaeger bomb, I drink it down quickly head out the door.

James came out from the drivers sit sprinting towards me holding my arm zigzagging to his car. Removing my blue strap heeled shoes James's face close to mine strapping my seatbelt on "your messy drunk but still cute" I am enormously giggling from my drunken situation I laid back and turn on my left side facing towards him his face close to mine I steal a smacking kiss on his mesmerizing blue eyes "you know I love your blue eyes they speak so much of you" curbing my knee up to my chin and James started to driving away and I fell asleep on the road.

Chirping birds along with the stillness of serenity in this sunny Saturday morning. My brain is spinning "aww my head hurts" I lean my head back on wall. James coming in the door wearing his blue robe holding a wooden tray "good morning sunshine breakfast is served" "I could have just gone downstairs James but thank you this is my first-time having breakfast in bed" placing the tray beside me "perfect" handing me the coffee "just what I need my head is killing me" a perfectly toasted bread spread with strawberry jam, soft scramble egg and crispy bacon and cantaloupe on a side, although my hangover is sure a struggle but I can't remember a simple happy breakfast like this in my growing years.

———————*IIIIIIIII*———————

There was a time when I was eighteen, I got outcast by my parents for getting pregnant at young age. I was still living in same compound with my family but got kick out form our main home; they made me move in a tiny one-bedroom suite which is located at the back of our main house. I feel blessed that my parents still gave me a roof over my head despite of my betrayal to them as a daughter. My mother never want us to get married since were too young then. But our parent decided we should live together for the reason they don't want my baby to born without a father. I was two months pregnant with our first-born son. At this moment, I stop going to university I must sacrifice my years of finishing my degree so that the father of my children can pursue his.

It change my life drastically at age of eighteen. My belly is growing fast I wake up at six in the morning I start cooking making rice, eggs, hotdog, and coffee while Zander prepare for school. When he leaves by seven in the morning, I kept going with my day doing house cleaning, washing a full basket of dirty laundry by hands, once done I do a little walk and sometimes our maid accompany me but often, I walk alone. By the time I get back home it's time to make dinner. This is not a routine I imagine myself at age of eighteen.

The day came our first-born son came out to the world it was most precious gift that heavens given to us. I have no idea of what to do becoming a mother, but I want to give the best to my son holding him tightly in my arms staring endlessly so tiny and fragile baby whom ill love and take care for as long as I'm living.

My son Jacob was only three months old. For no certain reason Zander decided to stop school making his own choice to stay at home take care of our Jacob. Having both of us staying home depending on and waiting for our parents will provide for us, and to our son is too embarrassing. So, under the heat of sun for two weeks I have been submitting twenty-five resumes in total and got one call for interview and luckily got my first job as a sales associate in a memorial gardens company.

Drenched from a long day field work fifteen minutes away from our gate I can hear the loudness of wobbly talks and roaring laughter's. The lawn is crowded with Zanders group of friends and while drinking he is sitting by the corner beside with a full twenty-four case of San Miguel beer and holding my innocent son in his right arm and smoking a cigarette on his left. Since I started working, coming home with unpleasant scene with other people with no care smoking freely near with my baby makes me furious. I carefully grab Jacob from Zanders arms walk straight home. After changing I feed and bathe Jacob, we both laid in bed turning his lullaby music on minutes later we both doze off.

It was two in the morning I got startled by a clanking plate from our kitchen. Jacob sleeping like an angel gently putting his pillow on both side for safety. I open the bedroom door a cold mist brushing through my face coming from our half open main entrance door. I took two steps and Zander sitting in the corner by the kitchen the beating of my heart accelerated I paused to where I stood my stomach is about to explode as I watched Zander folding a foil with his thick fingers a shiny glass fragments of crystalline rocks playing the lighter underneath the foil as the crystalline rocks dissolves Zander took the pleasure of absorbing the intoxication in his brain it was terrifying to watch. I run back to our room locking the doors behind me tears streaming down my face my whole-body nerves wrecking. holding my son in my arms whipping in silence "we are going to be alright anak, we will be alright". I can hear his terrifying voice talking to himself as he reached his satisfaction inhaling that evil toxic to his brain. It's a total horror I am trembling in fear of what he will do while under the influence of evil drugs. I lied down beside my baby held him closer to me, hearing him constantly knocking on the door I close my eyes praying, eventually after few aggressive knocking he stop and I never bothered opening the door.

———— *IIIIIIIII* ————

It was once a dream to be a June bride, but I had my wedding in the winter season in February and it was truly unforgettable. James proposed in September 2010, where he took me on a transformative five-hour hike to one of the breathtaking lakes in British Coumbia. It was my first outdoor experience, and it sparked a newfound love for the nature. Three exceptional lakes in one majestic mountain, a sight that left me in awe.

A three kilometer hike left me in absolute awe of God's magnifecent creation. The first lake was so serene and peaceful. The second lake is my absolute favorite among the three; the lake is emerald green and mountain has white color from the glaciers reflecting off the water. The water is so tempting that i took my boots off to dip my foot in -"oh my!it's ice cold!" I only lasted a few seconds before swiftly stepping out. After reaching the third lake at the very top of the mountain, I was breathless but glad I survived; I had never been on such a difficult hike, but it was all remarkably worth the effort.

It was an unexpected moment James had all planned. While we sat eating our ham and vegetable sandwiches and tossing a corona can to quench our thirst, he suddenly kneeled down with a blue jewelry box in his palm. As he opened the cute box, a gold diamond ring reflected to my eyes. "My love; will you grant me the privilege of spending forever with you?". My heart started beating fast, and tears started running down my cheeks. I gave a big yes!; the other hikers congratulated us as they stood to watch, clapping hands; I suddenly felt a little shy. We hugged each in tears of joy. We started our journey down, locking his fingers to mine.

Our wedding was simple, intimate, but memorable and beautiful event. My mom came all the way from new york for our wedding. Many members of James family came from different provinces to celebrate with us. Our very own pastor at church blessed our wedding ceremony. I made a journal for our guest to answer few questions. But one question that really touch my heart. That is *to draw on how the couple met.* To my surprise; everyone draw a smoking house; and a firetruck. This was the first time i met James; our staff housing almost caught fire, and James was a volunteered firefighter then. My heart is full of Joy knowing how our family and friends remembered the beginning of our love story.

This is the new chapter of my life. Waking up at seven in the morning with a chai tea in my bedside table, sweet lips kissing my face all the way down to my neck, chest, and leg he then says in a whisper while continuing his ritual body tasting "your breakfast is ready I will pick you up after work" before he leaves in a hurry a kiss in my forehead before heading out the door.

I determined to change my career path. In every resume I printed my goal is to get the front desk clerk job. One of a multi billion hospitality industry called me in for an interview. We were sitting inside one of the conference rooms she's smiling widely shaking each other's hands "thank you for coming" "thank you for this interview" silently flipping through my resume "I see your applying for the front desk position" I got energize by her question "yes I have two years experience with the job back when I was still in Philippines" "but you never had an experience when you arrive in Canada?" inhaled deeply "no, that's because I was sponsored during Olympics as a room attendant and tied with contract to work for that company alone" "I see" nodding her head closing the folder. She's looking at me straight in the eyes " If your interested I can hire you as a room attendant since you have long years of experience in this position" smiling brightly to her " thank you for the offer but I am looking for a chance to work in different department" "sorry but we don't have open position yet at front desk" I gladly smiled giving her a hand shake "thank you for your time but I'm sorry I have to decline your offer" she slowly stod up and gather the files "thank you if you change your mind I will have your file in my desk" I respectlfully nod and left the room.

James is outside waiting. Instantly sprinting towards me as soon as he saw me coming out the main entrance sliding door by the hotel lobby holding a box of chocolates. "How did it go?" locking his fingers to mine walking towards the car "hmmm, frustrating" we were inside the car he glance at me with a big question mark on his face "why?" I lower my head closing my eyes took a deep breathe then pause for a minute "this is the sixth time that I applied for a front desk clerk job and they all offer me a room attendant position how will I be able to get experience with the line of work if none of them are not giving me any chance" he reach to my face turning my head towards his "don't you think maybe you can try applying for a different company how about retail store I can see you be great in sales" bringing his charm out with his teasing smile "ohh I never thougth of that yeah why not I should do that" we were laughing out loud after such realization "ohh see I'm a good husband thinking this things for my wife" and we were laughing more loudly as he drove away.

I remember my past when I was still with Zander, I was pressured with the quota I needed to sell of memorial lot every month. This is the very first job I had. After working for six months with the company I was only able to sell three lots, so I made decision to leave and find a different work.

I arrived home finding Zander drinking with same group of faces everyday. walking straight passing by them I can feel him from behind following me carrying Jacob in his arm, as we came in the house, I carefully took my son who is been scrubbing his tired eyes then laid him in his crib.

After changing my clothes Zander sat by the kitchen waiting for me. I started washing the dirty dishes that piled up since our morning breakfast. He step closer "ahhhmm, you got paid today, right? Can I ask for three hundred so I can buy those guys more beers"? slamming the plate on the kitchen sink and it crack in the middle "didn't I texted you that I left my job? Buying milk for Jacob is more important than your drinking habits?!" I walk away from him but his too fast to hold me and grabs my arm "why do you have to react like that?" glaring in his eyes "because I'm tired! why don't you get yourself a job to sustain your own drinking and drug vices! Leave me out of it!".

My vision turned blurry in the same way Zander swinging my arm around to face him. I see an incredulous look in his eyes a sudden heavy burning daggering force on my chest as his leg hits my upper body made me flew all way splatting to the wall. My tears started rolling terrified from the strong force of hit every inch of my muscles trembling shaking in horror while I struggle to free myself from the devil's leg plugging me to the wall. And I was only nineteen years of age then.

We love celebrating our little wins either big or small. James ordered an expresso martini for myself, and he always loves his beers we tossed for my new career that I will surely enjoy and love doing.

"Cheers! To your new adventure" tossing his can of beer and my martini glass up in the air. "Thank you! I can't wait to start." On my fifth martini my head starting spinning and I can't stop laughing zigzagging on my booties James tightly wrapping his strong arms around my shoulders we trudge for ten minutes towards our hotel. We came in the room took our shoes off but never made it to our bed instead we throw ourselves in the couch.

Relaxing sitting with my knee up resting my chin to my knuckles. Our dining area is facing to a mesmerizing massive mountain I am looking out the window watching the beautiful big snowflakes; constantly falling; while sipping my warm chai tea. James handing me a bowl of cereal with coconut yogurt, fresh blue berries, and banana; my kind of breakfast. "Enjoying the view?"; as his lips damps on my cheek coming from a cold walk with his dog. I took a spoonful of cereal savouring every taste of nutrients it brings to my tongue; "yes, this is beyond amazing."

It's a powder snow on a Sunday. Sun is up and James and I are both off from work. James got up at seven in the morning went straight down to the garage waxing his skis.

I am still lying in bed when James came out from the shower, he was about to change for his ski clothes when I grab his right arm and push him in bed his tongue meet mine. I still crave more of him my tongue explore his neck, down his chest and the pleasure of tasting his strong abs while my right hands reaching to play his hard shaft. I arrived between his legs my tongue delighted licking a soft skin of his manhood. I swallowed it whole his screaming with gladness continued playing of him inside my mouth gently taking my time to fulfill my satisfaction then blow it off my mouth. The amusement of the enjoyment moment we shared makes me want all of him crawling on top of him spreading my legs in between his face his tongue rapturing my watering honey pot grinding in pleasure. He pushed me down to bed spreading my leg up entering his hard shaft to my cave of wonders moaning in glee while his sucking my chest thrusting hard and fast, we screamed in joy as we both reached our satisfaction catching our breathes as he laid his head to rest in my chest. "You're the best" saying out of breath.

———————///////////———————

I remain standing for twenty minutes at the edge of a tiny downhill slope trail holding on tightly to my poles. James taking off his skis walking back to where I'm standing "come on I'll catch you" stood at the bottom trail arms wide open "no I don't think I can do this" "it's ok you'll slowdown once you get at the bottom you can do it!" his frustrating tone of voice putting pressure on me; "James, this is my first time skiing I grew up in a country that zero snow existed, why don't I just take my skis off and put it back on in the flat surface"; James pulled off his ski pole sticking on a deep snow I can hear the flowing river on the side of the trail all the trees covered in white brings out the brightness of the whole beauty of the forest good thing were the only ones in this majestic backcountry trail skiing; then James stood beside me; "ok form your skis like a pizza" as I tried to move both my foot to form a pizza I started sliding down screaming with fear of falling so I stop. I immediately gave up taking off my skis; but James refuse for me taking it off; a sudden strong blow of ski pole hit my right leg; "just keep going! Don't take your skis off!" his impatient voice scared me more and him hitting my leg with his ski pole continued till all I can feel in my right leg is numb and burning swelling pain; "hey! Were supposed to be having fun here! You can't expect me to be able to ski when it's my first time doing this sport!" pushing him away from me.

"ohhhh I'm sorry I'm sorry!" hugging me tightly "I want to go home now!". Carrying my ski and poles walking back in silence towards our car. I immediately took off my ski pants scuffle up the stairs grab ice from the freezer; throw myself in the green leather sofa pulling my tights saw my right side calf of my skin started to color in purple and green putting the ice on the injury area. I lay there closing my eyes embracing the soothing feeling of the ice brings to my swelling huge bruises in my calf.

James came offering a glass of wine "don't talk to me I never seen this side of you, I can't imagine you would hit me like that your riducously unbelievable!" ; "I'm sorry ok; I didn't mean to" staring at him fiercely "go away! Stay away from me! I don't want you hurting me again! Leave me alone!". Quickly went up the stairs and lock myself in the room.

The long wait is finally over my children's permanent residency visa has finally arrived in the mail. The struggle for three long years of begging from their father to sign one document stating that he will give me the full custody of our children which is crucial for the application has finally in my hands; a hope that will bring better life and future to my children.

I Immediately booked my flight to Philippines in two days and I can't wait to bring my children over.

Coming to Canada. A cold snowy January James awaits at the arrivals area holding a bouquet of flowers and winter jackets. A warm welcome hug "welcome to Canada Jacob, and Alex James can't hide his excitement hugging my son and daughter. We first stop by to have dinner at one of the Japanese restaurants handing both my kids a plastic spoon and fork since they are not used to using chopsticks. "Lannga, finish your food please because it's three hours drive getting home".

Jacob sat by the couch drinking a coffee, Alex sitting beside him sipping orange an orange juice staring in bewilderment through the sliding glass door watching a huge snowflake falling. Every pine tress covered in white.

The sumptuous smell of the mixture of butter, flour, vanilla, and eggs lingered from the kitchen all the way to the living room. Four plates lining up in the black marble kitchen counter each has two pieces of pancakes almost size like the dinner plate. Topping them with fresh banana and strawberry sprinkled with powdered sugar. A strip of bacon and scrambled eggs with a maple syrup in the center table. "Mommy! the snow is so beautiful can I play outside?" her twinkling innocent eyes looking at mine "yes we all can go out and play after breakfast ok anak?" they both race to the table eating away. "Mom is there a rice? After pancake I want to have rice with bacon and eggs" I chuckled from his question "I knew you'll ask so I'm prepared" took the white steaming bowl from the counter placing it beside his plate "here you go" his delighted face drawn all over him. Sliding the window open peaking my head out "hey my love stop shoveling breakfast is ready" glancing up the window doing a thumbs up "ok ill be right up".

At the principal's office at the secondary school James and I handed the documents required for both to complete their enrollment for this mid semester. My next agenda is meeting with the school psychiatrists.

Rectangular white table scattered folders and documents at the side of a laptop. "Let me make a file for Alex" opens her laptop and started typing. She handed me a document "this are questions it's a bit long, this is going to be our guide on how we can better assist her" "ok thank you". I then end up sitting in that office for a long while answering every question with a heavy heart.

The school hallway full of laughter from students going into their respective classrooms holding back my tears. Watching a group of thirteen-year-old girls full of joy and chatting away each one holding their own favorite fashion magazine. My heart sank realizing watching my daughter growing up when she was nine, she can't count from one to ten, Alex learn to write ABC in the right sequence after she turn eleven.

When Alex was nine, I started bringing her to her psychologist such service like this is expensive in Philippines. I need to bring her for a behavioural therapy and occupational therapy twice a day every week. This time I work as a front desk clerk my salary alone is not enough to be able to continue Alex's therapy program.

I am blessed that my mother and dad supported me financially to keep my daughter's program going. Praying for her development to improve each session.

There are times when she has her moment, she doesn't know how to express herself. When this moment appears her way of expressing herself is by destroying things. Every time coming home from work it has been a daily routine for me to fix what Alex have destroyed; being in the house all day with her nanny. The tv room is her fortress I always find tear pages of books, CD's crack in halves, tv buttons are hanging out, holes in tv stand, cut paper from magazines scattered around and cluttered broken toys.

After hours of de cluttering next to do is cook for dinner. Before eating my meal, I must feed Alex first which means feeding her is following her around cause having her sit in one place is impossible to do, all through these years I have learned how to pick my battles with my daughter.

Chapter 5

Family & Hope

got down on my knees, crawling inside the walk-in closet and shutting down the doors behind me. Darkness slowly enveloped the tiny space. Sitting in the middle of the cold carpet, hugging my knees, painful tears started flowing. I hear the heavy snowstorm howling through the entire neigborhood at five in the afternoon. Frustrated and praying for mercy, I begged heaven to give me strength and wisdom to continue living. Problems attacked me all at once. I felt so exhausted I couldnt think straight; I was on the verge of losing hope with all the heavy circumstances I was going through, and I just wanted to end it all.

Once I had a simple vision when I have a family of my own. It doesn't have to be perfect as long as we have our Sundays as one family going to church and serving God together is a bliss. But sometimes life test you on the simplest things that you desire most.

I am sipping my red wine watching a trending tv series in Netflix when I got an unknown Philippine number randomly sending me photos. I can tell immediately that the scene is inside my brother's room. In the photo is a bald man standing near by the white wall holding a white long rubber swinging it in the air, two other men watching what his doing while my brother sat in the bed wearing black shorts without shirt zooming the photo at the edge of the bed I see syringes, foil pipes, and other paraphernalia's I don't recognize; surely I can tell all of them are high in drugs. I don't know what I'm seeing but it doesn't seem to sink in to me yet, but I have a bad feeling of what my brother and his group of friends are doing.

I can't explain the emotions within; with no clue who is sending the photo. All of a sudden, a dump of worries pouring all over me. Startled with James coming up the stairs soaking wet from skiing all day. "Hi. How was skiing? your bit late" taking off his hoodie "yeah I run to one of a friend I know from way back when I moved here, we went out for a couple beers" placing his ski boots and ski socks on top of the heater "that's good you need to hang out with your friends once in a while". Sliding my cellphone at my back pocket "dinner is ready made some chicken aftritada" placing a full plate in the table "thank you" touching his lips to mine "ok enjoy, I will go up in the room I need to call mom". James face turning sour swiftly he always have a bad feeling whenever I communicate with my family, running up the stairs dialing mother's New York number. I know she will not like the news I will tell her but she must know and need to be aware of her son's doing and help him get out of that evil vice.

The discussion with a mother and daughter about my brothers evil habbit was not well taken. Painful worries flowing over to both of us. We want to help him but all our worries ended up to nothing.

It's eight in the evening and snowing hard outside Alex is at the youth center where she likes to hang out after school. Normally I picked her up. We thought its better to train her to become independent but as her mom I always worry of her safety especially when dark kicks in.

Glancing at my tablet's time, it's nine thirty in the evening and it has been snowing heavily since this afternoon. I swing by Jacob's room: "Anak. come with me, please; we'll pick your sister. "No mom it's too cold out there". Inhaled deeply and exhaled my dissapointmen. I walk back to my room; James comes out from the bathroom, drying his hair. Grabbing my cellphone from the bedside table "who are you calling this late?". "I'm calling a taxi ; it's safer that way to pick Alex up", I say. In a blink of an eye, my cellphone was flying ip in the air; I jolt from where I was standing. James, roaring voice echoed to the room "It's a waste of money for taxi! just walk!" "I just want Alex to come home safe; it's heavily snowing out there!" with full of frustration, I say it out loud. James bolts from the clothing drawers, jumping on top of m; his burning palms are tight on my neck. His devilish face, which I have never seen in all the years we've been together, is terrifying. HIs palms tighten around my neck. "I can't breathe, James!" I utter, barely able to say the words; I'm grasping for air as fright crawls all over me. With all my strength, I kick his stomach, throwing him off me.

Catching my breath, I rolled out of bed as far away from him as I could. Every part of my nerves was wracked with fear. I pointed a shaking finger at him. "Don't you dare come near me, or I'm calling the police!" in that moment, James face lit up; he was awaken from his hellish behavior. "Ohh my God, Im so sorry. What have I done!" Unstoppable tears flowing. "Stay away from me!" I stprmed out the door, down the stairs, grabbing my winter coat and slamming the front door behind me.

After picking up my daughter we walk on a long route to get home safely. Putting her school things away and making sure she showers properly. Pulling the extra mattress from the storage placing it to my children's room laid it on the floor carpet "mom you're sleeping here?" Jacob's puzzled face watching me lying down in the twin size mattress in time that Alex finish from her shower coming in the room "yeeyy mommy you're sleeping with us tonight?" she immediately laid down beside me "yes baby" hugging me tightly " goodnight anak Jacob and Alex, I love you both very much" seconds later my daughter snoring beside me and my son peacefully sleeping but, I lied there eyes wide awake traumatized thoughts running visioning the horror incident with James.

I am losing my sense of direction day by day and I knew there was something in me that needed fixing, but I couldnt figure out what. I prayed wholeheartedly, pouring everything to the heavens asking why I felt so lost. I didn't know what was going in my carrer, family and my whole life was a total mess.

I finished work early and decided to head home immediately. Both of my children were still in school, and James was at work. I threw my heavy working bag onto the living room floor. With a mind racing, I ran up the stairs. I stormed inside the closet room. Bursting into tears. my body felt weak, and my heart felt like it was about to explode in anguish.

I heard my daughter's excitement coming from inside the house."Mommy!mommy! you home?" I wiped my tears dry, stood up, straightened my clothes, walked out the door as if nothing had happened. "Moommmm!" she called from downstairs. "yes! baby, I'm in the bathroom," I responded from upstairs. She gave me a sweet, warm huig and a loving kiss. Brightly smiling, she said, "Mom, I'm hungry." I laughed at her intro statement. "Okay, well me too". You're going to help me make dinner? how does chicken adobo sounds?" "yes, yes please". We ran downstairs, sprinting towards the kitchen, and started prepping.

It was perfect timing when James and my son Jacob came in the door together. ", dinner is ready," I said, holding a full plate of chicken adobo and placing it on the dining table. Jacob sniffed the air towards the kitchen, "hmm, that smells good mom." James passed us by, "you guys go ahead, Ill eat later. I can't stand eating with your children; they are parasites!" it was a painful word he blurted out of the blue without any consideration for how my children would feel.

A busy Friday at work preparing for the long weekendcoming up. While making a report for one of my trainees, my boss grabbed the side armchair sat beside me: "Alpha, how's everything?" I stopped taking notes looked at her in the eyes, and smiled: "Yes, Trish is catching up well, though it's her second day of training." My boss gently pulled my clipboard away and placed it on the table. "What I mean is, how are you?" she asked, pointing her finger towards my heart. It was a heavy, unexpected question, and I was not sure how to answer.

I'm holding back my tears; my heart sank all the way to the ground. "I knew something is wrong that's why I ask, she said calmly holding my right hand, even though you're not saying a word, I can sense that something is troubling you, come with me let's go to the office". She led the way to the office and I followed her inside.

"Whatever will discuss in here will remain in this room" say's Mandy with full of compassion. Streaming tears coming out my eyes; I have been holding for a while. "I don't know how to start I am not use to telling my personal struggles to others; asking help to anyone is something that I am not comfortable to ask. Mandy handing me the kleenex "take your time whenever your ready I'm all ears" sniffing in tears as I wiped it dry. "Are you willing to get a professional help?" I nod my head in agreement. Mandy started dialing a number and hand the phone to me. "I will leave it to you from here, take as much time you need come back to work whenever your ready" holding the phone with shaking hands "thank you" and the door slowly closing behind me.

Wednesday at eleven thirty rainy morning. I am at the waiting area patiently waiting for my turn at the counselling office. Being in a situation that's so new to me and doing something for the first time in your life feels strange. I was not sure what I'm supposed to do once I'm inside that room. My name finally called by the assistant my heart starts pounding coming inside the office. Very well accommodating she immediately stood up extending her hand "hi nice to meet you how are you?" shaking our hands "hello I'm not good I guess since I'm here to seek advice from you and how are you?" "ohhh I'm great here have a seat" pulling the chair fronting hers "ok I will ask questions and please feel free to tell me if your not comfortable to answer it's ok" reassuring me with her hand gestures as she speaks calmly and softly.

"So, why are you here today?" both my palms holding tightly on the armchair "I want to seek advice about my husband" taking notes to what 'm saying "ok, go on what about James?" I can't help but sobbing relentlessly "it has been two years I wanted to fix our relationship; our marriage; I have been asking him for so long that we both need a counselling" she continued writing on her paper; "but his not here, right?. A marriage is done by couple, but you're the only one who is here where is he? Is he willing to fix your marriage?" raising her eyebrows constantly staring at me; " how about taking a break a space between you two and if he tries to call don't answer it; so both of you can think, sometimes couple needs to separate so they can think" shedding more tears "he told me if I leave him he will kill himself and will leave a letter stating that it's my fault why he killed himself" swaying her pointing right finger "no, no, no that is not right you tell him, you will call police if he will do that".

"You know you should ask your son; I can see that in this whole situation his the one who sees all the chaos at home" silence for a minute "He was once divorce why do you think his first wife left him? His manipulative behaviour is choking all of you and it's making you so unhappy why don't you leave him?" "but, I want to fix us fix our marriage" "yes I understand but again his not here how can you fix a marriage when you're the only one who working on fixing it"; my mind began cloudy and can't think right "do you love him?"; a question I didn't think twice answering "yes!"; she stood up and firmly say "ok, then this will be our first and last meeting". I got lost by her statement she led me towards the door carefully opening "good luck to you" stepping out her office leaving that building with broken heart and full of tears.

The night was young and I was reminiscing the time when my grandmother use to tell me a bedtime story.

I was eight years old my grandmother and I sat in a long narra wooden sofa it's the third night continuation of the journey of Prince Juan. A story that has been passed on from generations to generations in our family. This story has stuck in my mind and heart. I remember sharing the story to my friends they gather around me at the side of the street watching each my friends focus on me listening eagerly to the adventures of Prince Juan and mimicking how my grandma does her every hand gesture and cutting the story short to continue it the next day. After having my two children I tell them the story of Prince Juan every bedtime.

My grandmother Lola Linda love's all her apo's my siblings and I grew up well taken cared of by our Lola. Both our parents were busy making money specially my Dad. As a certified public accountant my father working for the government keeps him busy day by day. And every weekend he spends his all day in his office catering clients after clients who owns huge businesses in town. So, my grandmother helps both our maid and nanny's to take care of us from home, to school to bed.

After when my brother and my younger sister we step high school my mother's sister took grandma in her home to help her take care of her another Apo. I felt sad to be apart from my grandmother, but I know I can visit her occasionally. Her bedtime story remained in me and lingered in my heart that I remember every word of how the story goes and keep telling this story to every apo and cousins I have. The story was pass on generation to generation in our family.

Every event when families get together all cousins and apo's gather around in the living room attentively listening to her; telling the great adventures of Prince Juan again and again.

It was eight in the morning I'm very excited for a new career. Here I am in a hurry preparing myself for a job interview. Blowing my hair dry dry when I got a viber call from my aunty from Philippines. "Hello aunty how are you?" A long silence on the line. "Hello;?aunty what's wrong?" I can sense the sadness in her voice as she finally speaks, in her whimpering tone saying "your lola pass away this morning" I drop my hair blower broken pieces scattered on the marble floor. "Nooo! No!" sobbing restlessly; sat in the corner of the bed wailing in tears.

James silently come in the door sat close to me wrapping his arms around my shoulders; "I'm sorry for your loss"; with no words to say I just sat still. After hours of crying, I lay down in bed with only robe wrapping around my body keeping me warm in the cold winter night I can feel my swollen red eyes, I just laid with a blank space brain until I fall asleep.

Two weeks later the job interview I have missed has been reschedule. I feel lucky for them being considerate and giving me another chance to get interview. Three hours before my interview I stayed in library sitting in front of a large glass window staring in space and praying silently in my head.

Inside the HR office sat and put a smile in my face though my heart is heavy knowing I can't see my grandmother one last time. Despite I was not emotionally ready my interview went on; but; sadly it did not went well. Every challenging situation I went through since Living in this wondrous place that's so full of adventure has shaped me to become better and someone I never expect or dream of becoming. Finding the right career for me in this amazing town where many people from all over the globe hunger to experience has lead me to create my own opportunity.

With my grandmother's passing made me feel so devastated that I can't see her one last time. One day while I sat at my favorite spot lighting my cigarrete where I can see the water running through a tiny stream surrounded with massive pine tress in this small park, all this tress have felt and witness every heavy burden and struggles I went through; in every changing seasons for the last fifteen years in Whistler; prayers; and being close to nature is my great comfort.

An idea came to my mind I wanted to do something for my grandmother and I remember the bedtime story the journey of Prince Juan, I want to bring the story to life. I don't know how and I don't have any clue how; since I have zero background in writing and I am not a writer I never dream of becoming one.

So day by day I go to the library and do my research. One struggle I will be facing is how to translate the story to english since it was told to me by my grandmother in our dialect; which is cebuano. I can speak english but crafting the words to make the story enjoyable for the readers or children is not a talent I have. But heavens seem to lead me to this career and through my devastation I have discovered a talent I never knew I had.

Here I was every days off from work. I spend most of my time doing research of how I am able to find a publishing company to bring my grandmother's bedtime story to life. I am not sure how these kind of process is done but I am googling every possibility of publishing company I find.

Keeping myself busy with this opportunity I am creating for my future career James and I don't seem to have time at each other his more happy going out in out door adventure and myself shaping my career path of the unknown. He came up to me one night while me and my children watching movie by the living room eating buttered popcorn. He sat beside me giving me a flyer of a certain event happening Whistler writers festival at fairmount hotel "you can sign up for this and meet other author's and writers" his blue eyes full of sincerity "ok thank you ill look into it".

It's a two week event where I can meet and learn to improve my writing journey. But one event I dont want to miss a chance is to meet publisher's and preach my manuscript; and hope they will publish my story. I don't know how to do it but without any hesitation I sign up for it.

Arriving at the hotel. Unexpectedly I was not alone being first time to do this event. Where all told to line up and only given fifteen minutes to present our manuscript to every publishers. I feel butterflies in my stomach at I am nearing for my turn. The lady in front of me with a curly long blonde hair asking me question; "so it's your first time too?" I nod my head "yes" and the four ladies behind me said it's there first time too.

We started introducing ourselves while waiting in line "I work as a teacher" the woman in front of me sharing her field of work "I'm a director of the hotel here in town" the lovely short brunette woman behind me "ohh me I'm retired" the one after the woman behind me "I run my own local shop here in town" the fourth woman answered and together this lovely ladies ask me "what about you? what do you do?" smile widely answered their question with great pride " I work at the liquor store as a sales associate". "Ohh nice I thought your face looks familiar; so thats where I have seen you then" slightly nodding my head "yeah I get that a lot with locals, asking me where they have seen me since I look familiar to them; I always say will at the liquor store thats for sure;" we all laugh "yep! one popular store in town where everybody gets to shop their essential" they all hilariously laughing.

The first room I came in a silver hair shoulder length hair sitting in front of a brown rectangular wooden table with a pile of manuscripts in front of her. "Hello how are you today?" reaching her right arm to mine "hi I'm great a little bit nervous since this is the first time I have attended this kind of event" "I see have sit" holding my manuscript to my chest "Ok so what work do you have for me" poured a glass of water handing it to me "thank you, yes so I wrote a childrens book, but I'm not a writer, I never knew I have a talent in writing even" she nods her head as she eagerly listens "this is the bedtime story that my grandma use to tell me when I was a child which has been pass from generation to generation in our family"; I sip water I can hear my heart pounding like a drum; "and I wanted to bring this bedtime story to life in memory of my grandmother"; I handed her my manuscript which she excitedly took and read "have you contacted a publishing company yet?"; scanning through the pages "In fact I actually have " "I am very willing to publish your book" she sits up straight looking at me in the eye "this is your dream, your journey, your story and your life" smiling at me "I like the uniqueness of your story" placing my manuscript in the table "have you sign any contract with the other publishing company?" I stop and think for a moment " Ohh nohh I think I might have" and to my surprise she handed my manuscript back to me "well that is sad I would love to publish it but if you have sign contract already then I'm afraid I can't published it, it's too bad all the best to your writing career. I let go of huge disappointment of exhale as I walk out the door. But her inspiring statement will be in my heart as I embark with this new adventure.

After one year; it was January of twenty seventeen Prince Juan got published. And I feel so blessed to be able to have a successful book launch supported by friends and locals in town. Since then I never stop enhancing my skills. As I keep moving forward to a better opportunities. I am led to a new talent that I myself is surprise discovering it. Becoming a writer and art collector are two things I never dream of becoming. But, here I am enjoying every journey it's leading me to.

Chapter 6

//

Dust from the past

A dust from my past and a divine sprinkle of hope in the future. To be exact; I was only twenty six years old then. It was dark. There was only one lamp post lighting the streets, and it kept blinking on and off. The only light guiding my way towards the house where Ineeded to go. Each step I took, my wedge got heavier as the mud piled up in the bottom of my sandals. Careful not to slip, my right palm leaned on na wall, sliding through the cement, with a smell of rotting and musty dead plankton as my arm held for balance. After reaching the placc, I found a small shack house. I stepped inside; there were four other women waiting, sitting on a wooden bench. My nose whiffed a strong chemical stink down my throat, almost making me puke. Holding my breath, I sat beside the others.

Minutes later an elderly grandma approaching me; she has a long white hair, "You must be Alpha" I nod my head "yes" gestured her hands for me to stand up. She's too quick putting her right palm touching my belly ; leaning her head towards my lower tummy as if she's listening what's inside. My heart flew like a bird as her fierce black round eyes *fixed to mine "ok you will be next after this woman behind you" she took a small bottle out from her dress pocket; spreading a slimy weird texture of oil it to her palm spitting some vodoo words on it that I can't understand, after she's done with her ritua;l she immediately undo my pant and wiping the slimmy oil all over my belly. I grasps on a deep breathe; as her warm palms touching my belly skin.*

As I sit and wait I close my eyes terrified of what I'm about to do. Coming here all by myself in this frightening decision. A part of me wants to walk out and run from the place but half of me also is telling me to be brave since my future lies in this decision I make; "ohh God forgive me" I kept repeating it in my head again and again.

My name was called I came inside a room; there was only one candle lighting the tiny space, with a tiny bed; she's sitting in a low black stool at the end of the bed. "Take your lower garments off" my whole body is shaking as I got instructed of what to do. "You can call me Lola Perla, your belly is only two months old so it will be a quick one" my body slantly sitting; she hold my legs wide open strapping it on each side of the bed. "This is going to be a lot of discomfort and it will be painful; you must endure it ". She took a long plastic tube inserted it inside of me I feel the tube moving inside of my lower belly. The weird movements inside me from the tube continued for about twenty minutes my tears flow as she continue what shes doing mix emotions storming over me "now breathe in I'm pulling it out now!" I felt something inside me rip as she forcelly pulling the tube out in me quick and strong.

Suddenly a strong liquid flowed out from my opening streaming to both my legs; letting it drip in a metal basin and a clanking sound fell out from my belly I turned my face away not wanting to see it and Perla immediately discarded it.

A pungent rich smell of the blood unfold the whole room I feel sick to my stomach. I laid for a few minutes; then she help me dress; my whole body suddenly felt weak, I noticed she place a large size of sanitary napkin in my underwear as she slip it up on me. Continued assisting me as I struggle to get up I slowly sat in the waiting area "rest for a while you need to gain some energy, walking from here will be not easy I will have one of my daughter assist you and get you home safely". This is a very dark nightmare experience I'm so full of guilt; and heavy conscience that is forever imprinted in my heart, mind and soul.

I called work and asked for two weeks off my blood never stopped flowing since that night. It came to mind that I should see a doctor but afraid to do so since our family is known all over town. I will be on the front page of news spreading all over the City of what I have done; I don't want to destroy my father's reputation. It was over a month till my body recovered and the bleeding finally stopped. Day by day after work I go by the church asking for forgiveness in my silent way keeping that horrible night by myself. One mistake I can never forgive myself. A year later I got called to come to Canada. The two years wait for my application has now come to light.

Looking back on my early years of marriage I was happy and content. It was a warm summer day James and I were inside a green Canoe floating. Despite the heat; the lake waters still cold. We were sitting on both ends of the Canoe. I love just to sit and stare at James lying with his gray shorts unbutton his blue polo shirt showing off his beautiful white skin and his favorite cap covering his face soaking up his body with the vitamin D and holding a sigle can of Corona beer. This is the only time I see him so relaxed and forgets all the problem in the world. In my head I pray that he will always be this relax and at peace. It's brings so much joy in my heart seeing him so chill and stress free. Once his anxiety kicks in he becomes a nasty, irritable and a total asshole man. And whenever his anxiety kicks in he always brings out the total worst out of me. I wish he can always stay the man I knew from the beginning; but fate doesn't work how you wanted it to be. I told myself back then; that I once have the best; I will never settle for less. Cause truly James is the best among the past relationships I've been. To be treated like a queen, is every woman's dream from a man.

Flashback came to my mind, there was a time while slicing bellpeppers in the kitchen counter James stood in front of me opening up a conversation. "I heard you talking to your dad a while ago how is he?" his palm scraping the vegetables crap throwing it all to the compost bin; "his alright as expected after hospitilazition he is going to have lot's of maintenance and his medicine is expensive" he suddenly stop what his doing "You need to stop sending money to them Alpha; we don't have any money"his statement felt like a loud bell to my ear hearing the same statement again and again for many years. And for many years I choose to ignore him saying these depressing statement. I slam the knife in the kitchen counters; "I'm so sick and tired hearing this from you for the last six years!" throwing the cutting board in the kitchen sink taking a huge exhale; for so long I never speak out; I always stay quiet and kept everything within me; " why you always speak and even embarrassed me in front of other people; just because of money?!" I am getting hysterical glaring at his face; my eyes about to tears; everything I have kept within me for so many years will burst out in this moment; "you speak that as if I don't have any right to spend the money! I work hard to earn; every penny and the money I sent back home is coming out from my own pocket not yours!"; he stood straight arrogantly speaking "ohh really?; sorry but were married and we are getting deeper in debt"; my tears flowingly bursting out; " you have that debt before I came into your life! why are you holding me accountable for that?!; and besides it's my Dad were talking about I am helping here!"; I turn around walking away from the person who gives me more stress daily, I storm up the stairs to our room slamming locking the door behind me.

After my book Prince Juan finally came to life holding the very first master piece I have created feels overwhelming. A classic bedtime story that is not only full of magic and wonders but also valuable memories brought back from our family heritage.

Tears of joy holding on to my very own work of art. Finally, I did it! a heirloom story in our family and honoring in remembering my grandmother. I took one hard copy and started writing a dedication at the back of the book cover a heartfelt message to one inspiration in my life, James. So, I laid the book by our bedside table to a wonderful surprise awaited when he got home from work.

It's already dark. I am still working on my second book project by our dinning area. I glance at my watch it's already eight in the evening his normally home by four in the afternoon I have been dialling his number for the last three hours but his unreachable.

My eyes got tired and sleepy and it was past ten in the evening I shut my laptop down and clean the surroundings leaving all my notes and journals out by the computer table to continue working on the project first thing in the morning. I poured myself a glass of red shiraz and went to the bathroom and prepare a hot bath.

Laying low in a warm steam bath. The soothing moist of the lavender bath salt swirling in the air moistens the bath room. Calmly sipping my wine a relaxation and moment of escape from my topsy-turvy reality lies in this tiny bath room. I heard the bedroom door opening James finally made it home at past eleven in the evening. Wrapping my bath robe on "hi mahal, you bit late how's your day?" taking off his working clothes and throwing them in the laundry basket; "there's a job I need to finish took so long to get it done" his sour tone says how his day went. "ok, well the bath still warm if you want to relax". I was about to give him a hug but he was quick to avoid me "no! I'm too dirty right now" walking pass me to the steamy bath tub splashing in. Something felt off but I just ignored it. I took a glance at where I had left my book but it had not moved even an inch. When I finally lay in bed I waited for him to get noticed he was about to open the drawer when he finally notice the book "whats this?" staring at the book cover flipping back and front "flip it open" the excitement I felt is flowing. My eyes sparks in the dark room that the one valuable person is holding my piece of art. As he reads my message I see nothing but a blank face. "Ohh you wrote it?" turning his head towards me with his blank face "ok, can we go to sleep now? I'm exhausted"; my heart sank for I was saving this hard copy for one most important person in my life and all I had is a downhearted reaction.

I waited for two days for him to at least congratulate me or even ask me how come he never notice I was writing. Too much of my disapointment I sent him a text message '*everyone who knew I'm able to publish a book was happy and proud for me; but you!? not even a simple congratulations! it wouldn't cost you a cent to say. But after message was sent in just a few seconds he responded 'ohhh sorry congratulations!'*. After reading his response my heart just fell all the way to the ground shattered into peices. Since then big or small accomplishments I never share to James anymore.

———— *////////* ————

Fall is around the corner we were in the deck James is cooking a bbq ribs and some corn. After a month I am able to publish my book James started asking me questions about it he began to get interested. It took him a month to absorb in his mind of what I have done. " You know what came to my ind lately James?, that it would be nice if I'm reading the book I published to our own child" he sprinted towards me holding my chin up staring at my face and started laughing in my face. "What's so funny?" agitated by his reaction "no! I am never going back to those stinking diapers not now; not ever!" I feel insulted; I immediately stood up and walk away with a shattered heart. I know deep within that I am being punished not to have anymore baby since I have comitted a unforgivable sin from heavens.

———————— ///////// ————————

It's mid month of December it finally snowed the whole neighborhood all covered in white and surroundings is so bright the scenery everywhere is pleasing to the eyes. This is the only time I find plowing fun when it's fresh powder makes scraping easy and light.

Flipping the last batch of pancakes I'm making for breakfast. The kids are playing on their gadgets. "Alright, breakfast is ready. It's a blessed saturday morning". Jacob, grab a plate fromthe counter. Alyssa, help set the table. "Here's everyone favorite maple syrup," I say, placing the bottle in the center of the table. James comes down the stairs in his ski clothes. "Morning, have some pancakes before skiing. "He places his ski pole by the wall, sits on the stair step, puts on his ski boots and says, "no, you go ahead, I don't like to eat with your with your children, they're slobs!". His words are like a thousand knives piercing my heart. I got lost for words; he immediately takes his skis and leaves in a hurry.

My children heard James painful words. I don't know how will affect them and not sure how to ease how ease their pain "ok kids don't mind what James said his just too crazy to go skiing" placing pancakes on their plates holding my tears back "ok let's pray before eating and let's pray for James too his probably going through a lot this days".

I remember when my grandmother is still alive she keeps repeating to me back then that karma will come in an unexpected moment in your life. I never understood it, until this moment. It marked in my head that this is my karma and the most painful to realize all of it is that, I'm not the only one paying for the sins I committed; but, also my children are suffering for it. I never felt so embarrassed, ashamed and unworthy of all the wrong doings I have done.

My son Jacob after graduating high school was slowly drifting away without realizing that our distance as a mother and son is drawing apart. I understand as teenager they become difficult towards their parents but in my heart I felt that his putting a wall between us.

It's two in the morning, for the last two weeks I can't sleep well. Helplessly worried of my son's decision. The conversation we had stick in my mind and it's adding a huge stress to me his firm voice resonating in my mind again and again. "I will marry her mom I don't care if it's you or the whole family is against it!". I guess this is what I have to pay being a single parent juggling schedules day in day out. I admit I have spent more of my time working and struggling to make ends meet focusing on the basic needs for my family making sure we have roof over our head, food in the table proper clothing for every season changes; it's a tough one because when we walked out the door from my ex husbands home we left with nothing else but our clothes, winter boots and jackets all pack in a black garbage bag; after the painful separation I totally struggle the three of us is back from scratch.

I kneel down at the edge of my bed pouring every hurt, worries, and painfully complaining to him "why must I be punish like this dear Lord?" tear's streaming I have been kneeling for hours whipping and whinning to God about everything why? why Lord? feeling like a lost child confuse, angry and hurt. My hours of solemnly whipping came to an end. I stood up firmly marking my heart the choice I made; to make it better for all of us. I know God is with me, empowering me to triumph over circumstances I face. Knowing he is in my life, I can conquer every obstacle, no matter how daunting or insignificant, because God's greatness surpasses anything in this fleeting broken world.

As a mother I want what is best for my children specially for my son. Among the two that heaven has gifted me, only my son has the ability to be able to survive when I'm no longer living. As the old saying goes mother always knows best. I may have lost the six years of not being there for my children; but in my heart I still know what is best for them.

It's been few weeks my son and I ignoring each other; it's most awful feeling as a mom. That your in war with your own child;

but I stand firm for I know his decision is wrong. Coming home always feels chaos the commotion is too much day by day. Our arguments and fights are worsening each day is turning out to be very exhausting.

I know it is not the right thing to pry on my son's personal messages but something inside me is telling me to check their conversation with this girl.

Jacob went for a basketball game. I went to his room found his cellphone in his bed. Slide it open and asking for a pin exhaled in frustration with no clue what his pin is. So I called his bestfriend hoping she might have a clue thankfully her guess is right.

On Jacob's facebook messenger I found their conversation with this girlfriend. My heart sank as I read every line from these girl who claimed to be a professional accountant. Her controlling and manipulative behaviour reminds me of my ex. and I feel so sad I don't want my son to go through the same toxic relationship like I did. As I scroll more taking pictures of every conversation it torn my heart piece by piece. How can someone treat my son inhumanely no respect, brutal words, cruel, sadistic, harsh and vicious statement from this lady crushes my son's spirit. Downgrading him in every conversation. I continued taking photos up till the last conversation. I did not raise my son to be treated in such torture. Messages lingered in my mind all through the night word by word circling one after another insulting words in my brain. Lying in bed for hours; sleep can't get through me; and I know I need help and I cannot do it alone so, I sat lean on my back towards the headboard staying still closing my eyes then heartily praying lifting up everything to heavens.

Whenever things gets out of hand and my life get's tougher I run to my Dad or Mom but I more talk to my Dad about anything. And this made me realize that in life no matter what age your at we still seek advice from our parents. Even though my dad is not an easy person to approach to.

One time I was already in my university years I ask his permission to go out clubbing with friends. "What time do you intend to go out and come home?" his calm manner when asking question like this is more alarming "tonight at ten dad is that ok? I'm not sure what time will be home though" with his legs crossed and right pointy finger on his lips thinking deep with my response "ok before you go I want to see who your with and I need assurance that they will take you home safely" I joyfully jump out of bed hugging him tight kissing him on the forehead "thank you daddy!" so excited that I got my father's approval rush to my room and started to change.

And just as my Dad empowered me through guidance and discipline, I strive to do the same for my son. I encourage his independence, trusting he'll make wise choices as long as I know who he's with and where they're headed. Before he heads out, I remind him "stay out of trouble, or else you'll be in double trouble when you get home", looking straight into his eyes to plant my words cleary in his brain and instill deep within his heart. Like every mother, if our child is happy, we are even more fulfilled.

My father is just a phone call away how much I missed him. Now I'm going through a tough challenge with my son. But, my only one mentor, protector, great adviser, my hero my dad was already taken away from me, from us, hoping his watching over us from heaven guiding us through our family conflict and chaos. Everything get's too much to handle by myself. I feel so alone and negative emotions slowly eating me.

Two months has passed our situation just gotten worst I blocked my son from the facebook since it's the girl manipulating his account and not talking at each other. I am having a hard time to restore our relationship and I can't accept the fact that by somebody who is miles away from us, our family is in total disaster..

Tossing and turning in my bed it's one in the morning I got a text message from my son saying only *'mommy'* my heart felt immediately that somethings wrong. I peak in his room and his not home yet I saw his other gadget in the side table slide it open and went to his messenger my eyes widened in horror as I saw the horrifying message from my son to one of his lady co worker *"sorry thats not me sending you indecent messages that's my girlfriend using my facebook account"* my heart beating fast scared of what the situation is *"belive me thats not me I swear I'm gonna kill myself so embarassing of what she did"* I kept scrolling and there I found that Jacob's girlfriend sent an indecent video of him and her to that co worker just because she's so jealous of why my son added her as a facebook friend. Her psychopathic jealousy disorder is beyond measure. Worried of he will hurt himself, I open my facebook messenger calling his co worker and friend I need to check his where abouts and he sent me a photo of them drinking in a club somewhere that he will bring Jacob home safely. I closed my eyes and thank God his safe.

One week after that incident happened Jacob lock himself in his room. I check on him calling him out to have meal together.

I waited for him to open up. "Mom Charmaine and I broke up, I can't stand her attitude anymore" I felt the heavy pain in his heart and I am hurting with him too in silence I never expected an quick answer of my prayers I feel so blessed and by his comfort and grace this painful experience will soon subside.

I told him "Anak pray and ask God to guide you to the right partner don't rush it will come in his perfect time". That night we all had a video call to all the family back home and that evening is another start of peace and harmony and love and joy in our family.

Chapter 7

Living the Gift of Life

Do you know that the gift of having a fullfillinglife is free to all of us?. During the time in my mid twenties young and innocent years. when were emotionally sensitive; always long for the love and support from our parents. But because our parents is so busy making a living the guidance and care is lacking. Yes, it is the stage where we are so full of adventure and wanting to try every fun we get and never missing out. But even then; we are still left feeling a meaningless life. Because of this emptiness that were lacking within; we start searching to fill that deep hole. We wanted to get valued and appreciated since our parent's are busy we then look for fullfillment from outside our homes. And once we became impatient of not finding that particular fulfillment; we start seeking in the wrong places; which leads us to make wrong choices.

When I was twenty-six years old, I made a life-altering decision to have an abortion. It never occured to me that it was a turning point or what it's transformative effects would be on my lifetime.

That pivotal choice was imprinted in me, and for many years I carried the weight of it's lessons every single day.

In these real world we live in when we make wrong decisions and choices. With the end result of it we bare the consequences or punishment on our own. But do you know it shouldnt be like that? You know there is always someone out there who has been with you all those times of your wrong doings, he never left you.

When I made that decision of doing abortion I could have died after that there could be a huge impact of infection and inflammation inside my womb cause I was so scared to have it check by a doctor, because my family, especially my father holds a great reputation being and accountant and lawyer back then. Once I get exposed then all my families reputation will get stained from my wrong decisions, so I managed it by myself to have it hidden for ten or fifteen or even more years. I managed to still be alive even at this point at age of fourty four. All those years God has blessed me even at that moment he carried me in his arms he was the one hurting most of what I have done to my boby. I turn away and forgot to run to him and ask for help in that crucial situation. But because his so merciful he saved me. because he created me from his own breathe he doesnt want me to become one of satan's minion and give me a purpose to live a life of having his holy spirit in me in every decisions I make I ask for his help and guidance.

I want to share my most turning point. It started on may 2023 I had a shoulder problem my doctor said it's a calcific tendonitis; and I must need to get a surgery immediately. It was not a life threatening to my health. It's a condition that even when you make a slight movement an excruciating stabbing pain lingers for a long time; it interrupts my sleep, even a drink of cup of tea is a hard to do, so I must learn how to do all my daily works with my left hand, and it is not easy when your a right handed person. As a single mother of two and one with mentally handicapped child is a pure struggle.

After a month of recovery I went back to my full time work. A part of the job I do is lifting, I managed to do my normal routine at work. But, four months after the excruciating pain came back this time more intense. I went to emergency went through many tests but every tests came normal. The Doctor tracing back the history of my surgery unfortunately they can't find the reason of what is causing the pain. I got prescribe with heavy pain killers which has always a strong effect on me. My Doctor advise me to be off work for another month and the month extended into two and ten months went by quickly.

The whole situation made me feel that heaven was punishing me. I was financially struggling. My struggles was far more worst during the COVID time. I stayed at home more and can't do all the regular chores at home.

One morning I struggled to get up my shoulder's is burning in pain, leaning my back on the headnboard closing my eyes and started praying. As I laid still in few minutes my shoulder pain started to calm down. The pain did not go away but the pain became tolerable. Every week I see my Doctor, and three times a week I have session with my physio. Things were getting more challenging each time and frustrations flooding in whenever Doctor and my therapist don't have answer of what really is goin on with my shoulder. Inflammation and pain comes hand in hand and right arm movements are going less and less.

Although I was fully determined to go back to my work fully, but my Doctor won't allow it since my arm is not totally healed yet. It was in the middle of summer afternoon after my phyiso appointment I went to sit in my favorite spot. The sun shining through the bench where I sit, facing the sun soaking up the warm touch to my skin. I close my eyes and praying in my head I felt the strong wind blowing all over me I opened my eyes and saw the green grass dancing beautifully along the wind and I close my eyes again this time the wind blowing stronger I continued praying in my head and ask "Lord what is it that you want me to do?". It was a click of the moment came to my thoughts telling me to read the bible. That moment I rushed home grab the bible and started reading. My hunger for his words started. I want more of him and be more of service to him. But I was not sure how. So I started to became more prayerful and putting everything I am going through in his hands and I realized that I finally found my secret place. By his guidance and grace I am found once again.

Every single day is a constant battle I face. Financially, emotionally and spiritually. In every storm we face that is over, there is always another storm comes in. with so many test I went through in life, one thing that I know of, I surpass all of them because I have a big God who lead me the way. I am so overwhelmed by his love and goodness. I am not good in speaking or talking about it, maybe that's why he bestowed me with a writing ability so through his gift I am able to share his grace to other's.

Because he created me and you from his own breath and molded me and you with his love and grace. His goodness is the most valuable gift we already possess since birth. So, day by day I always pray for a strength to fight every temptation to sin that is just lurking around me wherever I go.

In this temporary world we live in that is so full of distractions that will lead us astray. Even when we turn away from him he never turns away from us. By keeping him a part of him alive inside you he will always be there to rescue you in whatever circumstances you are in no matter how difficult no matter how big; because he is more bigger than what were going through. He died on the cross for you. Jesus paid it all. His sacrifice made me ask myself 'how can I be worthy of his love when all my life I failed him so many times and sinned against him massively countless times. But then here he is comforting me, blessing me and gifting me all the gifts I don't even deserve.

For many years I lost my way. And because he never once left me even at the darkest time of the choices I made. He deserves more than anything of my time a time spent with the Lord is the time I get to fixed that broken relationship for too long. I sing, I praise, I worship him everyday. He is my priority before anything else before starting my day. Everything around me becomes so light and calm even if I'm in the middle of huge storm because I trust his promise that is written (Jeremiah 29:11) "For I know the plans I have for you," declares the Lord, "Plans to prosper you and not to harm you, Plans to give you hope and future."

I was searching for a spiritual guidance and God lead me to a local church. A place where you are blessed with new family who are welcoming and willing to help you in your spiritual journey. I was once a member of the local church where I used to live for twelve years; but after my divorce and move to a new town, I lost connection with the Lord and to the church family I once knew.

It was 2013 when I accepted to follow Jesus and got baptist in a cold lake. I accepted Jesus my God as my saviour I never understood of having a relationship with our Father. My faith was very weak and it broke me down whenever I get attack.

June 12, 2024, is the experience I will never forget and can't put the right words on how to describe of what happened. I sat still in bed my back leaning towards the headboard praying seeking for his presence and face. I feel an invisible flow from my head all the way down to my body. The flow was so strong I opened my eyes and my thoughts wander. "What was that?" asking myself of the mysterious experience. I closed my eyes again and continued praying suddenly theres a light so bright and I don't know where the brightness coming from when its still so dark at five in the morning. I don't know what it was. But I can say that must be the holy spirit anointed me with his presence that he is there gladly listening to my prayers. Since then I look at every aspect of my problem in a blessed way.

Heavens never wants to bring harm to us, the devil does. Devil is full of schemes to destroy your strongholds. So, I keep my faith growing everyday so when he attacks me from all my sins I can fight against his trickery ways to fall from the devils trap. With God's divine and holy love for me I am able to resist all his evil plans.

Every where around me is so full of joy, love, peace and calmness. I never felt so light and everything seems easy even if I'm in a difficult challenging situation.

Whenever I make plans I pray for it first and wait for his response. If it is something he allows to happen then I go with it but if it is something he woukldnt allow I let it go. Before I push the things I wanted because I never put his promise in my heart and trusted him less. Now I claim his promise and take dominion for I know it is written that he will pave a better path for me and my family.

September 2024 after I came home from our membership class at church, I rush to the washroom to relieve the pea that I've been holding since our drive back. Startled to see a blood flowing out from me the toilet full of fresh red blood. I ignored it thinking it might be just my period. Then as the end month of September I am bleeding again this time more heavy and I need to sit in the toilet since it wont stop flowing. I rush to the emergency.

October 25, 2024 I went to see a Urologist. My partner and I went in the office sat and waited till the Doctor. came in the room I pushed my partner teasing him "I'm sure it's nothing and let's bet it's one of those doc check up's that he will give me advil" saying it loud and laughing at my own joke. Ten minutes pass Doctor came in "Hi I'm Doctor Thomas" extending his hands to me and to my partner "Hi nice to meet you Doc" he sat with my files in his hands "I will be honest with you your result is showing you have cancer of the bladder" at the moment I felt I did not hear him clearly turning my head to my partner "what did he say?" he holds on to my right hand tightly. "I will schedule you this thursday for further tests, do you have any questions for me?" I swallowed hard "No doc". My brain was totally empty and nothing else in my mind but the word bladder cancer. His making a mistake I don't feel sick or pain nothing at all except the bleeding.

First thing came to my mind *why Lord? is these some kind of a tests?*. We walked out that door both in silence.

I came home that night before going to bed solemnly prayed and believing in his healing promise. **Exodus 15:26 "For I am the Lord who heals you"** this scripture I hold dear in my heart. I trust his promise will happen. And because I refuse for a chemo theraphy I will follow where he will lead me for a natural healing. He created me so none of my body I own it's all his. As long as I will follow his lead I know he will fullfill his healing promise.

When you feel that your clock is tciking all of the sudden everything around you disappears and your only seeing the people important to you. For me that is my two children and my family. I only have my mom now and my brother and my sister. Every minute spend with them is a precious time that I can treasure in my lifetime it's a pure gift from above.

I never let my condition stop me from what lies ahead for me. Instead I use it to fuel myself to grow spiritually and finding time to spend with all the people he trusted me to tke care of even with my own struggles. That's the power of his grace flowing in us. The heart that is in constant fire for his presence. love, joy and peace and most of all contentment.

www.ingramcontent.com/pod-product-compliance
Lightning Source LLC
Chambersburg PA
CBHW021655120626
46545CB00002B/871